Shocking Celebrity Deaths and Murders

Dylan Frost

Contents

INTRODUCTION

Despite their wealth, fame, and power, celebrities are ultimately just flesh and blood like all of us. Their status or accomplishments are not a magical shield of protection when it comes to death. In fact, in some cases, celebrities are more vulnerable than your average person. As we shall see in this book, a number of celebrities have been murdered by their own fans. A number of celebrities have also been murdered in cases that remain unsolved. Fame can be a fickle and fleeting phenomenon and Hollywood is awash with former child stars who died in tragic circumstances when the phone stopped ringing and the money rang out. Our morbid fascination with celebrity deaths has existed since the early days of Hollywood. The infamous book Hollywood Babylon was one of the first volumes to cash in on this curiosity.

Hollywood Babylon is a trashy cult book about Hollywood scandals and 'secrets' from the 1900s onwards. It was written by 'experimental' underground filmmaker Kenneth Anger and first published in French in 1959. Anger was once a child actor and apparently culled together all the stories he'd heard and picked up about the darker and seamier side of the film industry, a world of 'cocaine-crazed comedies' and 'amoral extravagances'. The book, which was somewhat ahead of its time with its fixation on lurid tittle tattle involving celebrities, only appeared in the United States in 1975 after being banned in the sixties.

Hollywood Babylon is witty and morbidly compelling at times but not to be taken too seriously. Anger was desperate for money at the time he wrote it and it could be construed as a piece of experimental art itself rather than a legitimate book. Many of its claims have been completely debunked and the book is said to have created a number of urban myths that have no basis whatsoever in reality - like the story that the actress Clara Bow once slept with an entire American Football team. There are however plenty of strange tragedies and incidents in Hollywood and beyond which are verified and all too true.

In this book we will look at a number of celebrity deaths and murders. The cases that follow are eclectic and all darkly fascinating. Drug overdoses, murders, suicides, crazed fans, unsolved deaths, autoerotic asphyxiation, car crashes, freak accidents, drownings, disease, and so on. The book that follows is often dark and sad but hopefully a tactful read. While not sparing the details of these cases I have strived to also celebrate all the celebrities that are mentioned in this book. Many of the people that follow (the serial killers aside naturally) were very talented and often beloved. It is a great shame that many of them didn't live longer to accomplish more.

BRIDGETTE ANDERSEN

Bridgette Andersen was only seven years-old when she made her mark as a highly accomplished child actor in the film 1982 film Savannah Smiles. Savannah Smiles was a family film about a little girl who runs away from home. Sixty girls tested for the part of Savannah in the movie but Bridgette Andersen beat all of them to the role and was nominated for a Youth in Film Award for Best Actress. On the back of this success, Bridgette Andersen appeared as a guest on the Johnny Carson Show and acted in famous shows like The Golden Girls, Fantasy Island, Hotel, and Remington Steele. Bridgette Andersen was also in the short lived western sitcom Gun Shy. Around this time it would be hard to think of too many child actors in Hollywood who were as much in demand or appeared to have a brighter future ahead of them than Bridgette Andersen.

Andersen also appeared in television commercials and was soon drawing in a very decent income for her family. She also tested for the role of Charlie in the movie adaptation of Stephen King's Firestarter (this movie is a trifle forgotten these days but it was a pretty big deal at the time and was later a big influence on the popular Netflix TV show Stranger Things) but lost out to Drew Barrymore. This was slightly ironic because Drew Barrymore was one of the girls who lost out to Bridgette when they were casting the lead in Savannah Smiles. Bridgette Andersen and Drew Barrymore were rather similar in terms of their looks and talent so it was perhaps inevitable that they would often find themselves going up for the same child actor parts in the early 1980s.

In 1982, Bridgette Andersen also portrayed Mae West as a child in a television movie. Horror buffs might also note that Bridgette was in the 1983 anthology horror film Nightmares. Her later roles included the TV movie The Parent Trap II with Hayley Mills and an appearance in Beverly Hills, 90210. Bridgette Andersen worked all the time and was building a CV that most adult actors would happy to have - let alone a child actor. Andersen was not only talented but highly intelligent for her age. She read voraciously and even learned sign language for an acting part in the 1985 film a Summer to Remember. Andersen seemed like someone who would be intelligent and savvy enough to make the transition into teen and young adult roles when the time came but it was wasn't to be.

Sadly, like many child actors, Bridgette Andersen found that life in Hollywood was tough when she started to age out of 'cute kid' roles and become a teenager. Andersen eventually developed a drug problem and became completely estranged from her family. Acting work (which had once piled up on her doorstep when she was a little kid) was suddenly hard to come by and the telephone stopped ringing. Andersen studied theatre and ended up working in a health food store as she tried to get her life together and work out what to do next. Though she tried to kick her drug habit she was - tragically - not successful in this aim.

Bridgette Anderson died in 1997 at the age of twenty-one after a heroin overdose. She had been rushed to hospital in an unresponsive state and was eventually declared brain dead and taken off life support. The official cause of death was an accidental overdose from drugs and alcohol. Her last acting job had been in an independent film called Locker 28 but the film was never released in the end. Bridgette did make an appearance in a 1996 Pepsi Cola commercial which aired during the Superbowl but she is hard to make her out in the commercial. It is possible that she may have refloated her career in the end and staged an acting comeback but any chance of this happening was obviously destroyed by her drug addiction.

The story of Bridgette Andersen, sadly, was by no means new. Hollywood history is littered with child actors who went off the rails after early success and got into drugs. Bridgette Andersen was merely the latest. Ashleigh Aston Moore appeared in the 1995 film Now and Then when she was fourteen - for which she won a YTV Achievement Award. She had been acting since she was eleven and had also appeared in TV shows like Northern Exposure. Her last credit was an episode of Touched By An Angel in 1997. After that she drifted out of acting and vanished into obscurity. In 2007 she died of a heroin overdose at the age of 26. It seems that Moore, like a number of child stars who have fallen on hard times, tried to use drugs to fill the hole left by the loss of fame and an acting career.

Scotty Beckett was one of the kids in the popular Our Gang/Little Rascals series of shorts. He was acting from the age of four and signed a contract with MGM in the 1930s. His life rapidly went off the rails though - an all too familiar trope with child stars. He was arrested many times for drink driving, financial fraud, and was once caught trying to cross the Mexican border with illegal pills. He died at the age of 38 in 1968 after a suspected overdose. Brad Renfro was discovered at age 10 by director Joel Schumacher and cast in The Client with Susan Sarandon and Tommy Lee Jones. He went on to star in films like Apt Pupil and Sleepers. In 1998 Renfro was arrested for cocaine possession and in 2000 he attempted to steal a yacht from Fort Lauderdale harbor. Renfro had other charges for underage drinking and heroin possession. He died of a heroin overdose in 2008 at the age of 25. It was a tragic and all to familiar waste of a Hollywood career that had begun so promisingly.

Bobby Driscoll was the voice and model of Disney's Peter Pan and won a Juvenile Academy Award in 1949. At one point he was making $50,000 a year (with inflation that equates to half a million dollars today). Driscoll however, in a familiar child star trope, blew the money on drugs and couldn't get any work when he grew up. He died in 1968 and was buried in an unmarked grave because no one knew who he was or came forward to claim the body. It was only a fingerprint match from the police station that later enabled the authorities to deduce who he really was. There are countless other examples of doomed child stars and - sadly - Bridgette Anderson ended up part of this unenviable club.

It seems that Bridgette Anderson could never quite mange to extricate herself from friends who were a bad influence and facilitated her addictions. This ultimately cost Bridgette Andersen her young life. Because of her drug and alcohol abuse, Andersen looked older than her twenty-one years when she died. She looked tired and light years removed from the little girl who was a rising star in the early 1980s. Her ashes were scattered into the sea in Malibu.

JUDITH BARSI

Judith Barsi was a highly talented child actor in the 1980s and appeared in big productions like Jaws: The Revenge, The Land Before Time, and All Dogs Go to Heaven. She was especially good at voice acting and had no shortage of work in this field. Her home life was tragic though and she suffered domestic abuse from her unhinged and violent father. Judith's father Jozsef eventually killed both his wife and Judith before shooting himself. This happened in 1988 when Judith was only ten years-old. Judith's parents were Hungarian immigrants who had fled Soviet communism in their country (in the 1980s the countries of eastern Europe were obviously still under the control of Moscow and the Cold War had yet to show any concrete signs of thawing - though the days of the Soviet Union, unknown to anyone at the time, were numbered).

Judith was first noticed by a talent scout at a San Fernando Valley ice rink when she was five years-old. She was talented and charismatic. Judith appeared in over seventy commercials as a photogenic child actor. Judith's mother Maria was proud of her daughter and would always watch all of her commercials on television. Maria and Judith would excitedly sit on the sofa with celebration popcorn when a new commercial featuring Judith was due to air. Maria was even more proud when Judith began to be cast in movies.

However, there was a tragic cloud on the horizon in the form of Judith's father Jozsef. Jozsef was a heavy drinker prone to violent rages. He began to become paranoid that Maria might take Judith (who was obviously now the family cash cow and earning far more money than her father) and leave him. The attitude of Jozsef Barsi was curious and unfathomable. It was almost as if he was jealous of his daughter's success and resented her accomplishments. You'd think that his daughter becoming a successful actor would have made him proud and happy but this clearly wasn't the case at all.

Jozsef Barsi was an unpredictable and intimidating man with a bad temper. When you factor in the fact that he was often drunk one can see how nightmarish the home life of Judith must have been in the end. The domestic abuse suffered by Maria and Judith began to take its toll. Judith gained weight and pulled out her eyebrows. She was under great stress at home but still somehow attending acting auditions. Judith Barsi must have been exhausted and stressed in the end juggling her acting commitments with her awful home life. It is a great shame that Maria and Judith were not able to escape from his awful man or manage to tell anyone about their dreadful situation. That might have saved their lives but - alas - it never happened.

On July 25, 1988, Jozsef crept into Judith's bedroom as she slept and shot her in the head with a handgun he owned. He was likely drunk at the time. Ten year-old Judith was killed instantly. Maria rushed out to see what the noise was - whereupon Jozsef shot her dead too. Jozsef Barsi then spent two drunken days in the house where the dead bodies of his wife and daughter still lay. He then set fire to the house and went in the garage and shot himself dead. It could be that Jozsef Barsi only realised the gravity of what he had done when he sobered up. It was too late now. The damage had been done.

At the funeral for Judith, the actor Lance Guest, who played her father in Jaws: The Revenge, was one of the pallbearers. Many actors and children who had appeared in shows and movies with Judith attended the funeral to pay tribute. They were all shocked and upset by Judith's tragic demise. It was heartbreaking to think this talented little girl would never grow up now and that they would never see her again. It appears that no one outside the family was aware of how bad - and dangerous - things were at home for Judith and Maria.

Judith and her mother Maria were buried together at a cemetery in the Hollywood Hills. You won't be surprised to hear that Jozsef Barsi was buried somewhere else. No one knew where he was buried in the end and - to be brutally honest - no one cared either. The promising acting career of Judith Barsi was cut tragically short by this senseless and tragic act of violence and madness. Jozsef Barsi, for reasons that are hard to fathom, seemed to become increasingly angered and embittered by the success of his young daughter. This manifested itself in the worst way possible. The death of Judith Barsi is one of the most tragic and sad murders in the long and dark history of Hollywood.

JONATHAN BRANDIS

Jonathan Brandis appeared in his first commercial when he was four years-old and his family moved to Los Angeles to facilitate his career. He became a notable teen star and appeared in the TV miniseries Stephen King's IT (which is still fondly remembered thanks to Tim Curry's memorable and terrifying performance as Pennywise the Clown), The Neverending Story 2, and the TV show Seaquest DSV - in which Brandis played computer whiz Lucas Wolenczak. Seaquest DSV was produced by Steven Spielberg and a pretty big deal at the time although the show rather fizzled out in the end and was never terribly good. Don't ask me why, but I always remember Brandis for his part in the 1992 Chuck Norris comedy Sidekicks. In that movie Brandis played a bullied kid who dreams of being the action sidekick of the mighty Chuck Norris.

At the height of his fame, Brandis received four thousand fan letters a week and had to have security guards to protect him from adoring fans. Brandis was a clean cut looking kid and good at playing vulnerable or sympathetic characters. In his day he was one of the biggest teen stars in Hollywood. However, like many child and teen stars, Brandis found that when he got older his telephone didn't seem to ring as much as it used to. Once he began to age out of the teen roles that made him famous his career became less high profile and the parts were harder to come by.

There seems to no particular rhyme or reason to this phenomenon. Some child actors and teen stars make a fairly smooth transition to an adult acting career and maintain their status in Hollywood (one thinks of people like Natalie Portman, Scarlett Johansson, Ethan Hawke etc) while others inevitably tend to get rather forgotten. When he got into his twenties, Jonathan Brandis seemed destined to end up as one of those teen stars who ends up rather forgotten. He was no longer a big star and those days when young fans used to congregate outside the Seaquest DSV set to get his autograph suddenly seemed like a very long time ago.

Brandis did some TV and direct to video movies and was said to be annoyed when his scenes in the Bruce Willis film Hart's War were cut. Jonathan Brandis was a fairly private sort of celebrity by all accounts. He didn't lead the sort of crazy hedonistic party lifestyle that other young people in Hollywood were known for. Like many of the characters he became famous for playing, Brandis was quite sensitive and shy in real life. He had a small circle of friends and was anti-drugs - though he did drink too much apparently near the end of his life. Brandis was clearly prone to depression and the extent of this depression was (in hindsight) obviously hidden from his closest friends.

In November, 2003, Brandis was found hanging in the hallway of his Los Angeles apartment in what was clearly a suicide attempt. He was taken to hospital but declared brain dead and taken off life support. Jonathan Brandis had killed himself at the age of 27. His death was a great shock to those that knew him. They never dreamed his spirits were this low because he had always seemed cheerful and funny to them in person. Jonathan Brandis left no suicide note so his death remains mysterious. It was reported in the media that Brandis killed himself because he was depressed at the way his career had fizzled out and not lived up to early expectations. This theory, on the face of it, seemed as good an explanation as any for why he taken his own life.

The theory was disputed though by the actress Danielle Harris (who is best known for her horror roles and the Halloween movie franchise). Danielle Harris knew Brandis for ten years and was one of his closest friends. She said that Brandis had no depression about his career at all and was still working steadily. Brandis apparently wasn't that bothered about securing acting jobs anymore and wanted to move into writing and directing anyway. It appears that depression and mental illness was behind the suicide of Jonathan Brandis rather than worries about his career. It is a great tragedy that he was never able to talk to anyone and get the help he patently needed. His death was a great shock to eighties and nineties kids because they had essentially grown up with Jonathan Brandis watching him on television.

TED BUNDY

Ted Bundy was born in Burlington, Vermont in 1946. Bundy is probably the most famous American serial killer of all time. Ted Bundy is often considered to be the first celebrity serial killer in that he gave television interviews and looked more like a game show host than a deranged killer. Bundy was born Theodore Robert Cowell. He got the name Bundy when his mother married a cook named Johnny Culpepper Bundy. Bundy grew up thinking that his mother was his sister. Ted Bundy's aunt said that, when he was a child, she once awoke to the sight of Bundy carefully placing knives around her sleeping form. Ted Bundy was a Peeping Tom as a teenager and also got into trouble for car theft. His elan in stealing cars was something he used to his advantage in his various prison breaks later in life.

Bundy's first official victim was killed in 1974 but he may have killed for the first time in 1961 when he just fourteen. An eight year-old girl named Ann Marie Burr vanished from her Tacoma home in August of that year. At the time, Ted Bundy was the Burr paperboy and lived only four blocks away. Ann Marie's mother later became convinced that Bundy was responsible for her daughter's disappearance but Bundy never confessed to this crime. Bundy was said to have been seen in a construction ditch shortly after Ann Marie disappeared and his uncle was teaching the girl to play piano at the time. All of these details seemed more than mere coincidence.

Ted Bundy was ultimately rejected by his first girlfriend Stephanie Brooks. Bundy said he felt socially out of depth with

Brooks. She had brown hair parted in the middle - which obviously led to the theory that Bundy always sought victims who looked like Brooks. Ted Bundy went to the 1968 GOP convention as a delegate for Nelson Rockefeller. It is often suggested that he might have done quite well in politics. What he really wanted to be was a lawyer. He seemed to spend most of his life as a law student although - to his dismay - he was never that smart and found academic life a struggle.

Ted Bundy met a single mother named Elizabeth Kloepfer in 1969 and they had an on/off relationship that ran to 1976. Kloepfer later wrote a book about her life with Bundy. She loved Bundy and wanted to marry him. At first she thought the police suspicion of him was ridiculous but - gradually - she began to have doubts. Ted Bundy was always kind to Elizabeth Kloepfer's daughter. He would sing her lullabies at night. Bundy once worked as the Assistant Director of the Seattle Crime Prevention Advisory Commission. Ted Bundy also worked for the Department of Emergency Services (DES). This was a government agency that searched for missing women. When he worked for the Seattle Crime Prevention Advisory Commission, Bundy was involved in producing a pamphlet for women on rape prevention.

Bundy would spend a lot of time away from home and it was in 1974 that his activities as a serial killer began to spiral. Bundy would get women into his car by wearing a plaster cast and pretending he needed help carrying some books. One of Ted Bundy's other ruses for getting women into his car was to (with his familiar plaster cast on) pretend he needed help carrying his ski equipment. If you ever wonder where Ted Bundy got all his plaster of Paris from, the answer is simple. He used to work in a medical supply depot. Ted Bundy loved the Volkswagen Beetle. He even stole one of these cars once when he was on the run. The theory is that Bundy liked this car because it was easy to take out the passenger seat and thus easier to get a body into the car and hide it.

Ted Bundy had a custom of killing in the headlights of his car or during a full moon. He liked to see exactly what he was doing. Ted Bundy said that after he killed a woman, he would sometimes shampoo their hair so they had less of an odour. He would have sex with the bodies until decomposition made this impossible. The victims were usually stored in the woods so that Bundy could go back and visit them. Bundy called the part of him that murdered the 'entity'. When Ted Bundy was first at large, the police said they were looking for a man in a Volkswagen Beetle. This didn't really zero the search in on Bundy at first though because the Volkswagen Beetle was a very common and popular car at the time. In order to abduct women from parks, Ted Bundy would wear tennis clothes as if he had just stepped off the court. He would also pretend that he had a sailing boat.

In 1974, a woman named Carol DaRonch had a remarkable escape from Ted Bundy. At the Fashion Place Mall in Salt Lake City, Bundy pretended to be a police detective and told DaRonch her car had been broken into so she she went to the car park with him. Bundy managed to get DaRonch into the car and cuff one of her hands but she managed to get a door open and fight him off. Bundy pulled out a gun but DaRonch - who was obviously terrified - managed to flee. Carol DaRonch later testified against Bundy after his failed attempt to abduct her. People who knew Ted Bundy simply refused to believe he could possibly be a killer at first. These people included the crime writer Ann Rule - who worked with Bundy at a crisis hotline trying to talk people out of suicide. Rule said that Bundy even used to walk her to her car each night after work to make sure she was safe.

Bundy was responsible for the brutal murders of a number of teenagers before the failed abduction of DaRonch. The net was beginning to close though. He was picked out in an identity parade and the police found a ski mask, handcuffs, rope, and a pantyhose mask in his car. Elizabeth Kloepfer, Bundy's girlfriend, had also found plaster of Paris and female clothing in Bundy's possessions. Bundy was charged with the DaRonch kidnap attempt and sentenced to fifteen years in prison. They then managed to connect him to a murder but there was a strange interlude when Bundy jumped out of a window at the Pitkin County Courthouse in Aspen and became a fugitive for several days before being captured again.

Incredibly, Bundy then escaped again by hacksawing through his cell bars and making his way through a crawlspace. He then took the spare clothes of a member of the prison staff and managed to get as far as Chicago. After he escaped from prison, Ted Bundy ended up in Florida where he supported himself by stealing credit cards. He rented a room and pretended his name was Chris Hagen. After he escaped from prison and made his way to Florida, the authorities didn't have the faintest idea where Ted Bundy was. He could have remained undetected for years if his compulsive urge to kill hadn't got the better of him.

In January 1978, Ted Bundy broke into a dorm at Florida State University and attacked four students. One was throttled with a nylon stocking and another was found dead with her nipple bitten off. Another victim had a broken jaw. Bundy left but then attacked a woman several streets away so brutally she was left with a fractured skull. Kathy Kleiner, who survived Ted Bundy's attack on the Florida University Chi Omega sorority house, never went back to the college to finish her studies. When she picked up her stuff from the dorm a week later she noticed there was still blood on the wall. Before his attack on the dorm at Forida University, Ted Bundy hung around the campus and drank in some student bars. He was essentially doing research for his attack and also looking for any stray students he might be able to isolate and abduct.

After the Chi Omega attack, Ted Bundy stole a van and fled. He tried to abduct a 14 year-old girl but her older brother (thankfully) interrupted the abduction and chased Bundy off. Unbelievably, while he was on the road after the Chi Omega attack, Ted Bundy actually met up with a woman for a date. She obviously didn't know he was a serial killer. She thought he was a nice man named Chris Hagen. Ted Bundy's last victim was twelve-year-old Kimberly Leach in 1978. He raped and murdered her in Lake City, Florida. Bundy was not known to target children and it is speculated that Kimberly - tragically - was simply the only victim Bundy could isolate at that time. Ted Bundy's orgy of terror in Florida, and his career as a serial killer, came to an end in the early hours of February 15, 1978. A Pensacola police officer named David Lee noticed the car driven by Ted Bundy suspiciously pull out of an empty car park at one in the morning. Lee verified that the vehicle had been reported stolen and arrested Bundy.

During his last trials, Ted Bundy, acting as his own lawyer, completely shot himself in the foot by asking witnesses too many questions about the specifics of the Florida attacks. This served not only to remind the jury of the awful and graphic nature of the attacks but also made Bundy look creepy because he appeared fascinated by the gruesome details. The conclusive evidence against Ted Bundy for the Florida attacks came from the fact that he had bitten one of the victims on the buttock. Bundy had a chip in one of his teeth that was a perfect match for the bite mark. At his last trial in Orlando, Ted Bundy put his girlfriend Carole Ann Boone on the stand and proposed marriage to her (which she accepted). Carole Ann Boone was a deluded woman who, contrary to all evidence, refused to believe that Bundy was a serial killer. The pair actually had a child together in Bundy's last years. The daughter of Ted Bundy and Carole Ann Boone was the result of a conjugal visit to prison. The prison guards were bribed.

Bundy was fund guilty and sentenced to death. Ted Bundy fought a lengthy battle to avoid the electric chair. This was ironic because his refusal to plead guilty and insistence on defending himself simply made the electric chair more likely. Bundy only became confessional in prison when he sensed that the electric chair was looming on the horizon. He hoped that if he rationed out information about victims and burial places the authorities would decide to keep him alive. It was described as a 'bones for time' strategy. When she found out that her boyfriend Ted Bundy was a serial killer, Elizabeth

Kloepfer asked him if he had ever been tempted to kill her. Bundy said that he had thought about it once but would never have gone through with it. In one of his last interviews, Ted Bundy blamed pornography for the dark path his life had taken. It felt like a weak excuse to say the least.

Bundy died in the electric chair in 1989. Ted Bundy's last words before his execution were to pass on his love to friends and family. He was 42 years-old. A large collection of people gathered outside the prison when Ted Bundy was executed. They got drunk and let off fireworks. It turned into a big party. According to one of the guards in prison, Ted Bundy could hear the noise from this party. Ted Bundy's brain was removed after his execution. Medical tests concluded that it showed no sign of abnormality or injury. Bundy requested his ashes be scattered over Washington state's Cascade Mountains. This is where he buried some of his victims.

Bundy is suspected of killing many people than we can verify. He confessed as much before he died and admitted that he would never confess to all of the killings because they were too 'close' to home. By this he is presumed to have meant that the victims were neighbours or maybe very young. Bundy said that taking a life made him feel like God. He was addicted to the rush and sense of power it gave him. He was truly one of the coldest and most prolific serial killers in American history and all the more chilling because of the charming mask of sanity that he could project to an unsuspecting society.

GARY COLEMAN

Gary Coleman was a familiar face on television from 1978 to 1986 thanks to his role as Arnold Jackson in the sitcom NBC Diff'rent Strokes. The show was about two African-American boys from Harlem taken in by a rich white Park Avenue businessman and widower named Phillip Drummond (Conrad Bain). Coleman's famous catchphrase in the show ("Whatchu talkin' 'bout Willis?") was much imitated by seventies and eighties kids. The show seemed be something of a curse for its three main young leads - Coleman, Todd Bridges (who played Arnold's brother), and Dana Plato (who played Phillip's daughter Kimberly). Coleman, Bridges, and Plato found it nigh on impossible to get acting work after Diff'rent Strokes and were all beset with numerous personal troubles. Bridges is the only one of the trio who is still alive - which is pretty amazing when you take into account his own highly troubled history with drug addiction.

Gary Coleman had nephritis - a kidney disease which stunted his growth and made him still look like a child even when he became a mature adult. He could probably have played Arnold Jackson for decades without appearing to age much - though it obviously didn't come to that in the end and Coleman probably would have considered that a fate worse than death. Although the show was very popular, Coleman never cared for Diff'rent Strokes much himself and couldn't wait for it to end. He thought Diff'rent Strokes was dull and conservative and grew to dislike the long working days spent shooting the show. Diff'rent Strokes was notorious for special episodes where a social issue (like drug abuse, alcoholism, racism, and even child sexual abuse) would be explored. Gary Coleman really hated the preachy 'issue of the day' tone of Diff'rent Strokes.

There were a lot of famous guest stars in Diff'rent Strokes. Muhammad Ali appeared in one episode and Nancy Reagan (who fronted the Just Say No drugs campaign) was in the anti-drugs episode. In hindsight that was pretty ironic because in real life Todd Bridges and Dana Plato both went on to take enough drugs to sedate a herd of elephants. As for Gary Coleman's festering dislike of the show, he especially hated the fact that he had to play the same character - a smartass kid - for several years. By the end of Diff'rent Strokes, Coleman had grown to loathe the show.

Legend has it that by the end of Diff'rent Strokes, Coleman would sometimes refuse to say Arnold's famous catchphrase because he was so sick of it. Coleman was eighteen years-old by the time Diff'rent Strokes came to an and resented the fact that the production team still treated him like a little kid. In mitigation though he still LOOKED like a little kid so maybe they just forgot sometimes that he had grown up. In 1989, three years after the end of Diff'rent Strokes, Coleman had to sue his parents and business manager for dipping into his earnings and trust fund. Coleman had made $50,000 an episode on Diff'rent Strokes from the age of thirteen so this trust fund was a sizeable nest egg. He never spoke to his parents again after the legal case. The successful legal action netted him $1,280,000.

The legal case was a familiar story in Hollywood. Coleman was not the first child star to grow up and find his money gone and he probably won't be the last. Take the case of Jackie Coogan for example. Coogan was one of the most popular child actors of Old Hollywood and appeared in films like The Kid, Oliver Twist, and Tom Sawyer. He is believed to have earned around four million dollars as a child actor. However, when Coogan turned twenty-one he tried to access his money and found that his parents had spent it all.

Coogan took legal action against his stepfather and mother and although the money was gone the case did lead to what is known as the Coogan Act. This is a law which states that studios must set aside 15% of a child actor's earnings in a trust fund which no family member has access to. This law protects child actors from parents and family members who think they are entitled to take everything the child earns and have no plans for the future (when the child will be grown up and might not even be an actor anymore). Coogan continued to act and later secured one of his best known roles when he played Uncle Fester in the 1960s television series The Addams Family.

Gary Coleman, like many child stars, found that adult life in the entertainment industry - and ordinary life in general - was no bed of roses. His acting career was effectively finished as soon as he became an adult. No one wanted to hire a 4'8 actor who still looked like a chubby child. Coleman was hopelessly typecast as Arnold Jackson but that was the sort of role he was too old to play now. By 1999, Coleman had blown his money and was working as a security guard after being declared bankrupt.

Gary Coleman was clearly not a happy man. He was famously bad tempered and once punched a woman who asked him for an autograph. He required regular dialysis treatments and his health declined. He married a young woman named Shannon Price near the end of his life but it was a rather fractious marriage it seems with many fights and arguments. Gary Coleman suffered an epidural hematoma after a fall in 2010 and died at the age of 42. By the end of his life he was reduced to comic cameos or eighties nostalgia talking head shows. It was a far cry from the late seventies and early eighties when he was one of the most recognisable faces in America. It seems that Gary Coleman didn't cope very well with the immense fame that came his way at an early age. The rest of his life was plainly a struggle. This all seemed to leave him embittered and angry.

BOB CRANE

The seemingly clean cut Bob Crane began his career as a radio DJ and was later the star of sixties/early seventies sitcom Hogan's Heroes. The show was about Allied prisoners of war in Nazi Germany who are always up to various schemes and secretly trying to help the war effort for the Allies. Though popular at the time the show is pretty dated today and arguably of dubious taste. The show ended in 1971 and Bob Crane's career hit the doldrums soon after. He had a new TV show but that was axed after only thirteen episodes. Crane then appeared in a couple of terrible Disney movies in the 1970s called Superdad and Gus which have been understandably forgotten.

What torpedoed Crane's chances of regular work for Disney (or anyone else for that matter) was his private life. Bob Crane was, to put it mildly, a bit of a sleaze in real life. He was a sex addict and would pass around explicit photographs of the latest women he'd been intimate with. As you might imagine this sort of thing didn't go down too well with film and television executives. They say appearances can be deceptive and that was certainly the case with Bob Crane. He looked like a conservative, clean cut middle-aged man and yet in private he was acting like some debauched rock star.

It was just as well for Bob Crane that he had a percentage profit share deal from Hogan's Heroes because by the late seventies he was struggling to pick up work (maybe he was too typecast after appearing in a famous show years ago?) and doing cabaret and regional theatre. This meant he had to travel around a lot. Crane clearly didn't mind this at all because it gave him a chance to meet women. Crane's secret private life was facilitated by his friend John Carpenter (not the famous director, this was another John Carpenter) - who worked as a video salesman. The duo would trawl strip clubs and dingy bars looking for women to pick up. Carpenter supplied Crane with video equipment and the pair would make amateur porn films with the women they had picked up in clubs and bars. Crane had been making home sex movies since 1956 by all accounts.

Crane's private life almost certainly had an effect on his marriages. Around the time of his death he was going through his second divorce. It's hard to believe that many women would want to be married to Bob Crane once they became aware of his grim lothario secret porn life. In June, 1978, Bob Crane was found dead in a motel room in Scottsdale, Arizona. He was 49 years-old. Crane was in Scottsdale appearing in a play called Beginner's Luck. Bob Crane had been beaten to death with a camera tripod and had an electrical VCR cord tied around his neck. His face and head was smashed in so badly that it was difficult to identify him.

There was 'brain matter' on the wall from the impact of the death blows and blood all over his face. It was a brutal murder. The authorities believed that because of the force of the blows which killed Crane a fairly strong man must have been responsible. There was no sign of a forced entry - which obviously indicated that Crane might have known the murderer and willingly let him into the room. The actual murder weapon had been removed and was never found.

There was a glass of scotch on the bedside table but Crane didn't drink scotch so this added a layer of mystery to what was obviously a violent murder case. Around fifty videotapes were later found of Crane having sex with various women. The biggest suspect in the case was obviously John Carpenter. The day that Bob Crane died, Carpenter had been seen with Crane having lunch and the pair had an argument according to a waitress who served them. Crane and Carpenter were pretty close because they even sometimes appeared together in the same home made sex videos they made with all these women.

The night that Bob Crane was murdered, Crane and Carpenter had gone to a local nightclub together but they did not leave the club together. The two men both left separately with women they had met. The woman Crane left with though apparently did not go back to his motel room. What happened to Crane between leaving the nightclub and his murder remains a mystery. John Carpenter was eventually investigated and put on trial for Crane's murder. The police had found it especially suspicious that Carpenter had flown to California a few hours before Crane's body was found. Specks of blood and even brain matter were found in Carpenter's car.

However, Carpenter was found not guilty at a trial and DNA evidence tested decades later seemed to possibly confirm his innocence. The bizarre death of Bob Crane therefore, for now, remains a mystery. It appears to be plausible that Carpenter killed Crane (he was clearly the prime suspect) but the DNA evidence collected by the police was simply never convincing enough for a conviction. If there is any doubt at all in a case this serious the defendant obviously can not be found guilty and that's exactly what happened here. John Carpenter died of a heart attack four years after his last trial. He doubtless took any remaining secrets to his grave.

There was still money in Crane's wallet when he was found dead so this ruled out robbery as the motive. Theories as to who killed Bob Crane include the suggestion that a jealous boyfriend or husband of one of the women he picked up might have killed him. Another theory is that one of the women he had sex with found out he was secretly filming her and became enraged when she found out. We simply don't know for sure. A 2002 film called Auto Focus is based on Bob Crane. It's worth watching if you are interested in this bizarre true crime case.

DAVID CARRADINE

David Carradine was a prolific film and television actor best known for the TV show Kung Fu and the Kill Bill movies by Quentin Tarantino. Carradine had appeared in literally everything at some point or other although he never really became a huge star. He was more of a cult actor and was happy to appear in B-movies and oddities whenever his career hit a fallow stretch - which was quite often. Carradine was a rather eccentric actor who was difficult to assess. He could be absolutely terrible but if you gave him decent material he could be surprisingly good. You might say that Carradine was sort of like B-movie television version of Nicholas Cage in his day. He just kept working in anything to hand and left others to decide if he was any good or not. Carradine battled substance abuse and addiction in his life and this perhaps explains why he could never quite get to the top table of Hollywood A-listers.

In 2009, Carradine found himself in Bangkok to make a French film called Stretch. Three days before the end of shooting on Stretch, Carradine was found dead in his room at the Swissôtel Nai Lert Park Hotel on Wireless Road, near

Sukhumvit Road. He was 72 years old. David Carradine was found hanging in a cupboard. He was naked and had rope around his neck. The death was judged not to be suicide but as a result of autoerotic asphyxiation.

Autoerotic asphyxiation is among the strangest and most dangerous sexual kinks. It basically involves starving oneself of oxygen to heighten sexual arousal. It is, to say the least, a very risky practice - especially if someone is alone and nearly everyone is alone when they indulge in autoerotic asphyxiation. Those who seek an oxygen deprived high for autoerotic asphyxiation will put plastic bags over their head or partially strangle themselves with a belt or rope. It has been estimated that around 1,000 people a year die in the United States of autoerotic asphyxiation but it isn't something that is discussed very much or that well known.

Autoerotic asphyxiation is what you might describe as a very embarrassing way to die. Relatives of victims - for understandable reasons - tend not to be in a rush to talk about it. Famous people who have died in the act of autoerotic asphyxiation include the Australian singer Michael Hutchence and the British politician Stephen Milligan. Milligan was found wearing women's underwear with an orange in his mouth. The young British television presenter Kristian Digby is also believed to have died as a result of autoerotic asphyxiation. In 2010, Digby was found dead in his bed with a plastic bin liner over his head.

Though early reports on David Carradine's death cited suicide two autopsies were conducted (one involving the celebrity pathologist Pornthip Rojanasunan) and concluded that the death was not a suicide. Two of Carradine's former wives also admitted that he was into bondage and what they described as dark sexual practices. All in all it was a pretty grim and sordid way for this famous actor to go out. The story was all the sadder for the fact that he was making some obscure film (that few people were ever likely to watch) far from home. Alleged photographs of David Carradine's dead body appeared on the net after his death - which was obviously very distressing and annoying to his relatives and friends. Carradine did at least have a more dignified send-off in Los Angeles. Hollywood stars like Tom Selleck and Lucy Liu attended his memorial service to say farewell.

JACK CASSIDY

Jack Cassidy was an American singer and actor who won great acclaim for his work on Broadway. He appeared in everything from Hawaii Five-O to Mission Impossible and was in the movie The Eiger Sanction with Clint Eastwood. I always remember Cassidy the most for his terrific performances as the villain in two great episodes of Columbo with Peter Falk in the 1970s. Cassidy was a bit of a ham but his larger than life presence and natural charisma always made him enjoyable and polished to watch onscreen. He was a fantastic singer too.

Despite all of his accomplishments though, Jack Cassidy - much to his annoyance by all accounts - ended up becoming most famous for being the father of teen pop sensation and Partridge Family actor David Cassidy. There was a window in time where David Cassidy was probably the biggest teen idol in history. David Cassidy, at the height of his fame, could go anywhere in the world and get instantly mobbed by hordes of screaming teenagers. David's fame far outstripped that his father in no time at all and one can probably understand how Jack found this rather difficult to swallow after toiling away in the entertainment industry for years.

Despite the poise and calmness he could project onscreen, Jack Cassidy was a rather troubled man in private by all accounts. He was secretly bisexual (despite being married) and suffered from mental health episodes. Neighbours once found him mowing his lawn naked in the middle of the day. On December 11, 1976, forty-nine year-old Jack Cassidy returned home to his west Hollywood apartment after attending some parties. The parties were presumably early Christmas events as the festive season had nearly arrived.

Jack Cassidy was probably quite sozzled after this night on the town and the parties. His apartment took up the top floor of the swanky building he lived in. At around 5am Jack Cassidy felt asleep on his sofa with a lit cigarette. The consequences of this impromptu snooze were tragic and devastating. The apartment was soon in flames and many firefighters were called out. Friends desperately hoped that Jack wasn't in the apartment at the time of the blaze but sadly this obviously wasn't the case. It was Jack himself who had started the blaze in the first place.

The emergency services found one solitary body in the charred remains of the apartment. The body was burned so badly that Jack Cassidy could only be identified by his dental records and the wedding ring he always wore. Cassidy's face, nose, ears, eyes, and skull were burned beyond recognition and his body was reduced to a charred husk. It was a terribly gruesome scene. The official cause of death was cited as 'Extensive Thermal Burns of Body'. You probably didn't need to be Quincy to have worked that one out. Jack Cassidy was much liked in Hollywood and his strange, sudden, and awful death came as a great shock. Many actors attended his funeral and his ashes were later scattered in the Pacific Ocean.

BARBARA COLBY

Barbara Colby was an American actress known for her comedic flair and toothy smile. As a young woman she studied acting (which included a spell in Paris) and then won plaudits for her work in the theatre. She made her Broadway debut in 1965. Her first major television break came in a 1971 episode of Columbo and she went on to appear in a number of television shows which included The Odd Couple, Gunsmoke, and Kung Fu. In 1975, Colby played a prostitute named Sherry

Ferris in two episodes of The Mary Tyler Moore Show. Colby was a very good scene stealer and had good comic timing.

Barbara Colby's career seemed to be starting to take off by this point and it didn't seem far-fetched to think that she might soon have her own sitcom or start to pick up parts in movies. Colby was married twice and had homes in New York and Malibu. She had a pretty good life. Colby was into Vedanta and spirituality. This kept her grounded and down to earth. She also loved psychics and tarot readings. She believed in karma and reincarnation.

On July 24, 1975, Barbara Colby was on her way home after teaching an acting class in Venice, CA. She was with a colleague named James Kiernan. As was their custom, they stopped the car in a parking lot and took a break from the long drive. Apparently, this was a tradition for Colby. She liked to take a break and talk about acting with whoever was with her on the way home. While Colby and her friend chatted, a van approached containing two men. The men shot Colby and Kiernan once and then drove away. It was a random and senseless drive by shooting. The shooters didn't even attempt to rob the victims. One of the bullets had hit Colby in the chest and damaged her lung. She almost instantly died of the injuries. She was only 36 years-old.

Kiernan was taken to hospital and managed to give a description of the shooters to the police before he too died of his injuries. Despite the police having a description of the shooters the murders were never solved and no one was convicted for the deaths of Colby and Kiernan. Some men were arrested but it transpired they had nothing to do with the deaths and so they were set free. It appears that the murders were completely random. The men in question didn't even know they were killing a celebrity.

At the time there was a huge spike in these sorts of incidents in Los Angeles with homicides and drive by shootings going through the roof. Colby was just desperately unlucky to be in the wrong place at the wrong time. She shouldn't have stopped in that part of town but then hindsight is a wonderful thing. Colby obviously had no way of knowing that stopping for a break in a car parking lot was going to come at the cost of her life.

Barbara Colby's last role was in a 1976 television movie called The Ashes of Mrs. Reasoner in which she starred with Charles During. Colby was murdered three weeks before this movie aired on television. Colby was cremated and her ashes were scattered in the Pacific Ocean. Celebrities and co-stars like Mary Tyler Moore, Cloris, Ed Asner, and Cloris Leachman attended the funeral service. At the time of her death, Colby was playing Liz Erskine in the sitcom Phyllis - which was a sort of spin-off from The Mary Tyler Moore Show. Liz Torres took over the role after Barbara Colby's sad death.

JEFFREY DAHMER

Jeffrey Dahmer was born in Milwaukee in 1960. He was destined to become one of the most famous serial killers in history. Relatives of Jeffrey Dahmer say that his personality seemed to suddenly change after he had hernia surgery at the age of six. Dahmer became very interested in taxidermy and decomposition. Jeffrey Dahmer's chemist father taught him how to preserve animal bones. He was a very bright kid and had an IQ of 145 as an adult. However, he developed a drinking problem at a young age - which seemed to blight whatever potential he had. Dahmer was also gay and so all of his future victims would be men that he had picked up or developed a friendship with. When he was growing-up, Jeffrey Dahmer once stole a mannequin from a store and kept it in his bedroom. He had a sexual fantasy where he dominated an inert lover. This fantasy was by no means uncommon when it came to serial killers.

Dahmer said he first had a fantasy about killing someone when he was in high school. He is believed to have killed for the first time when he was eighteen. Dahmer murdered a hitchhiker he had picked up by hitting him with a weight. Dahmer used acid to dissolve the body and crushed whatever bones were left with a hammer. After dropping out of university, Dahmer became a combat medic in the 8th Infantry Division and was stationed in West Germany. Two soldiers who served with Dahmer claimed that he sedated and raped them in Germany. Jeffrey Dahmer was eventually kicked out of the army for his drinking though. After he was discharged, Dahmer went home and worked in a chocolate factory before moving in with his grandmother. Dahmer began to pick up men and there were more incidents of him sedating and sexually assaulting victims.

In 1987, Jeffrey Dahmer woke up in a motel with the dead body of a man next to him. He somehow managed to get the body out of the motel using a suitcase and took it to his grandmother's home (where Dahmer lived) so that he could dissect the body and dispose of it. Soon after, Dahmer moved into an apartment and his killing spree began to spiral out of control. Jeffrey Dahmer said he tried to stop killing but it was a compulsion he just couldn't ignore. Jeffrey Dahmer's apartment was so eventually so full with victims and body parts that he put one body in the bath and had to shower over it. The apartment contained a plastic drum of acid where three human torsos were dissolving.

Jeffrey Dahmer poured acid into the head of a victim named Konerak Sinthasomphone. Sinthasomphone escaped and wandered the streets in a daze. Tragically, some policemen who found Sinthasomphone then took him back to Dahmer's apartment after Dahmer told them Sinthasomphone was his intoxicated boyfriend. Dahmer was so crazy that he thought if he injected acid into a victim they would become a compliant slave for him. Dahmer would sedate his victims by giving them a drink that was laced with sleeping pills. Dahmer once drank the spiked drink he had laced for a victim by mistake. He passed out and when he woke up the victim had robbed him and left. Naturally, Dahmer didn't bother to report the crime. The 'thief' had no idea how lucky he had been that Dahmer gave him the wrong drink by mistake.

Dahmer is most famous for the fact that he would eat parts of his victims. Jeffrey Dahmer fried the body parts of his victims in a skillet before he ate them. Dahmer used a meat tenderizer to make human flesh more edible. During his police confession, Jeffrey Dahmer was asked if he ate human body parts plain. He replied that he ate them with salt & pepper and steak sauce. Neigbours of Jeffrey Dahmer did complain about the smell coming from his apartment once. He apparently told them that his fridge broke and some food went bad. Dahmer had a tray at the bottom of his fridge to collect the blood that dripped down from body parts. Jeffrey Dahmer would sometimes make sandwiches for neighbours in his apartment building. It is therefore possible that his neighbours might have unwittingly eaten human flesh. Dahmer liked to paint human skulls because he thought this made them look fake and they would be less suspicious if discovered. He used formaldehyde to preserve body parts.

Jeffrey Dahmer was captured when a man named Tracy Edwards managed to escape the handcuffs Dahmer had put on him and go and fetch some police officers. Dahmer had two hands and human genitalia in his kettle when the police searched his apartment. This was merely the tip of the iceberg. One of the police officers later described Dahmer's apartment as like entering a real life horror museum. It was very grim and disturbing. The police found a complete skeleton in Jeffry Dahmer's filing cabinet and three human heads in the fridge. Dahmer seemed relieved to have been caught and spent hours giving them a full confession.

In his confession, Jeffrey Dahmer said that when he cut up his victims he would remove his clothes and place the victim in a tub. He said he felt brief remorse for the victim but this did not last. Mostly, he felt excited. When he was captured, Jeffrey Dahmer told the police that he retained the skulls and bones of his victims because he wanted to use them to construct a place of meditation. Dahmer said that, circa 1983, he tried to use religion to fight off his desperate urge to kill. It obviously didn't work.

Dahmer was tried in Milwaukee for 15 counts of first-degree murder. The death penalty was not an option in the state so Dahmer was sentenced to life behind bars. He did some interviews while in prison. Despite the gruesome and unfathomable nature of his crimes, Dahmer seemed alarmingly normal and mundane in interviews. He was articulate and soft-spoken. Dahmer didn't serve much of his sentence in the end. In 1994, another prisoner (a convicted murderer named Christopher Scarver) attacked Dahmer and another inmate named Jesse Anderson with an iron bar after some sort of altercation.

The attack was so violent that Dahmer later died in hospital. He was 34 years-old and the life of one of the most infamous serial killers in American history had ended. Want some trivia that will never be of any use to you? When the police searched Jeffrey Dahmer's apartment he had VHS tapes of Return of the Jedi, The Exorcist II, Chippendales Tall Dark and Handsome, and an episode of The Cosby Show.

JILL DANDO

In the 1990s, Jill Dando was one of the most recognisable and famous faces in Britain thanks to her duties as a newsreader for the BBC. Dando also hosted Crimewatch (a show which highlights unsolved crimes and appeals for fresh information) and the travel show Holiday. Jill Dando was literally all over the place. She was one of the most high profile presenters in the country and everyone knew who she was. On the morning of 26 April 1999, Dando was shot dead outside her home in London. She was 37 years-old. The killer had shot her in the head and fled the scene. It was a shocking and baffling murder. Why on earth would anyone want to kill Jill Dando? That was to prove a question which rather perplexed the police.

After a huge police investigation (which naturally dominated the news headlines in Britain) the police arrested a local oddball named Barry George. George lived about a mile away from Dando. Barry George was a loner with learning difficulties. He was an odd character but being eccentric does not make one a criminal or murderer. If we were to allow the police to arrest all eccentric people then half the world's population would end up behind bars! Most of us are eccentric in our own ways. In 2001, Barry George was sentenced to life in prison for Jill Dando's murder but it was a conviction which troubled many because the evidence seemed far from conclusive.

The police case against Barry George was dubious at best. They made great play of the fact that firearms residue had been found on his clothing but this was later proven to be so minuscule that it proved nothing. Half the population of London might be found to have a minuscule speck of firearms residue on them from brushing against someone on public transport. The police also noted that Barry George had newspaper articles about Jill Dando in his flat. Given that George was a mentally troubled hoarder with about ten million newspapers in his flat it would have been impossible for none of these newspapers to mention Jill Dando because she was one of the most famous people in the country! Once again the police evidence proved nothing.

The biggest problem with the police case against Barry George is that the murder was highly efficient. It was done very quickly and the killer was very elusive in escaping from the crime scene without detection. Barry George was a shambles of a man who could barely tie his own shoelaces. It beggared belief to think that he would have been capable of this Mafia style assassination. George was clearly no angel. The police found evidence that he was something of a peeping Tom and sometimes followed women. There was no conclusive evidence that he was a murderer though.

After three appeals, the conviction of Barry George was quashed in 2008 and he was set free. This now begged an obvious question. If Barry George was innocent then who had really killed Jill Dando? There were a number of theories. Because she had hosted Crimewatch (a show which is all about catching criminals and solving crimes) there was an obvious theory that an embittered criminal might have killed Dando in revenge but this theory didn't stand up to much scrutiny and failed to supply any significant leads.

A former IRA member claimed that Dando had been killed by an IRA hit squad. While the IRA would doubtless have been capable of such an act this claim was never verified or proven.

The police had obviously scoured through Dando's past and private life to see if a scorned lover might potentially be responsible and have had a grudge against her but this also failed to provide any notable leads or lines of enquiry. The most plausible theory is that Jill Dando was killed in connection with the situation in the former Yugoslavia. Dando had fronted a television aid appeal for Kosovar Albanian refugees and only days before she was killed NATO had bombed Radio Television of Serbia's (RTS) headquarters - killing numerous journalists. The general theory then is that Dando was killed in retaliation for the bombing of Radio Television of Serbia's (RTS) headquarters. RTS was like Serbia's version of the BBC - for whom Dando worked. It was an eye for an eye revenge killing (according to the theory).

The 'hit' on Dando was what you might describe as professional in that she was killed quickly and efficiently and the perpetrator fled the scene in swift and elusive fashion. This suggested that the killer was a trained hired professional and not some lone nutcase. Arkan, the Serbian warlord, is alleged to have been the person who ordered the hit on Dando. He died though so it would impossible to question him about it now. Despite the apparent Serbian connection, the police never actually sent anyone to Serbia to investigate and still stubbornly refuse to accept this theory might be true. The investigation into the murder of Jill Dando therefore remains open and the actual truth has yet to be proven.

ALBERT DEKKER

In 1968, Albert Dekker was a veteran and much respected 62 year-old actor actor who had recently appeared in Bonanza and The Wild Bunch. Dekker had been appearing on the screen since 1937 and was a suave and distinguished looking man whose roles included East of Eden (with James Dean), the sci-fi horror film Dr. Cyclops, and the film noirs Kiss Me deadly and When Killers. When he went missing for a few days and failed to turn up to some appointments, Dekker's worried fiancée Jeraldine Saunders (who, to take a slight detour for the purposes of gratuitous trivia, created the TV show Love Boat) had his apartment door unlocked and found a very strange and unpleasant surprise.

Albert Dekker was dead in his bathtub and dressed in bondage gear with a noose around his neck. There were leather straps around his chest and rope binding his ankles. He had a ball gag in his mouth with pieces of metal chain tied round his head. His skin (including his buttocks) had obscene lipstick graffiti scrawled on it and there were hypodermic needles sticking out of him in various places. A vagina had been crudely drawn on his stomach. Jeraldine Saunders said that this grim and grisly scene haunted her for the rest of her life. It must have been a terrible and awful shock.

The official verdict was on Albert Dekker's death was accidental asphyxiation while attempting autoerotic asphyxia. However, there is a lot of dispute about this and many at the time believed that verdict was preposterous. Many believed this was a simple case of robbery and murder. Money

($70,000 in cash - a very sizeable sum in 1968) and camera equipment was missing and it seemed unlikely that Dekker could have written all over his body himself. How could he have scrawled on his own buttocks with lipstick? It wasn't impossible but given the amount of graffiti and the elaborate nature of the bondage gear it seemed questionable that he could have done all of this alone.

Jeraldine Saunders was convinced that Dekker was murdered and his friends never believed the bondage autoerotic asphyxia theory either because they thought it was completely out of character. Paul Lukas, a fellow actor and friend of Dekker, said - "Al never would leave the world in such a terrible shambles. He was a man of culture and breeding."

Believe it or not, the police originally (and preposterously) ruled Dekker's death as suicide. That would be a rather convoluted and strange way for someone to commit suicide! If he had decided to commit suicide then why did Dekker leave himself in such an embarrassing and strange situation for someone to find? That didn't make any sense.

It is believed that the police found S&M toys and porn in Dekker's apartment - which may have been a factor in leading them to the autoerotic asphyxia theory. There was no sign of forced entry in Dekker's apartment - which obviously must have been a factor in the police not ruling this a case of violent robbery. Jeraldine Saunders (who died in 2019 at the age of 95) believed though that the missing money and camera equipment meant it must have been a robbery which then turned into murder. Her theory was that the assailant must have been someone that Dekker knew and willingly let into the apartment. Dekker's son Benjamin had his own theory. He believed that Albert's death probably came as a result of a sex game gone wrong with a secret lover - who was presumably male. The secret lover must have fled the scene after helping himself to money and valuables.

DOMINIQUE DUNNE

Dominique Dunne portrayed the teenage daughter Dana Freeling in the classic 1982 horror film Poltergeist. She had also been cast as Robin Maxwell in the television miniseries V (this popular miniseries was about seemingly humanoid and friendly aliens who come to Earth and turn out to be blood-drinking lizards who want to take over). Dunne was the sister of the actor Griffin Dunne (who was best known as the time for An American Werewolf in London) and her father was the famous journalist Dominick Dunne.

Dominique Dunne was very much a rising actor in Hollywood. She was attractive, intelligent, and ambitious. Poltergeist had put her on the map and V seemed destined to make her much more famous.

Dominique Dunne looked a bit like a younger version of the Raiders of the Lost Ark actress Karen Allen and appeared to have a very bright future indeed.

Around the time that V was in pre-production and about to start shooting in 1982, Dominique Dunne was twenty-two years-old and in a relationship with a chef named John Sweeney. This relationship had become quite intense and claustrophobic and Dominique Dunne decided she wanted to end it. John Sweeney was a volatile and clingy sort of character and Dominique was beginning to find the relationship very constrictive and stressful. It could be that as her Hollywood career was now taking off (1982 saw her appear in big TV shows like CHiPs and Hill Street Blues) she felt she had outgrown Sweeney and no longer wanted to be tied down to a relationship at such a young age. John Sweeney though was not a man to take no for an answer.

Sweeney arranged to meet Dominique Dunne in a residence they used to share and begged her to give him another chance. She refused to do this and insisted that their relationship was over for good. Dominique Dunne was adamant and wanted to move on with her life. Her plans no longer included John Sweeney. Sweeney was so enraged by this that he snapped completely. He became incredibly angry and throttled the actress for what was later determined to be at least four minutes. Dominique Dunne passed out unconscious on the driveway after being strangled by Sweeney. She was put in a life support coma after being rushed to hospital. Dominique Dunne never recovered and died four days later.

On the fateful day she died, Dominique Dunne had agreed to talk to Sweeney in the porch belonging to those she was living with. She had a friend in the house (the actor David Packer - he was actually rehearsing scenes for V with Dominique Dunne when Sweeney arrived) but he agreed to wait inside. Packer later rushed out when he heard what sounded like smacks and screams. Sadly it was all too late. Packer found Sweeney kneeling over the unconscious Dominique Dunne. Sweeney told him to call the police. It is said that Sweeney made a failed attempt to kill himself with pills before he was taken into custody. This was disputed by the Dunne family though.

One might think that this was a pretty open and shut case of murder. John Sweeney had plainly strangled Dominique Dunne to death. To the amazement and anger of the family of Dominique Dunne though, John Sweeney was convicted of voluntary manslaughter and only served three years in prison. It felt like a ludicrously light punishment for what appeared to be a clear case of murder. The trial was something of a farce. For reasons best known to himself, Judge Burton S. Katz seemed to be biased towards the defence and wouldn't even allow testimony from the Dunne family about Sweeney's abusive treatment of Dominique. Sweeney claimed that he had gone to the house that day because Dominique had agreed to get back with him. He said he only got angry when she told him that was a lie designed to hurt him. The Dunne family were angered by this claim. They knew that Sweeney was making this all up.

John Sweeney claimed he had been distraught when Dominique collapsed and rendered medical assistance. The Dunne family disputed this too and said Sweeney had been calm and collected when Packer found him. Sweeney was acquitted of the murder charge and found guilty of manslaughter. Judge Burton S. Katz then added insult to injury by saying this was "a case, pure and simple, of murder. Murder with malice." Well, if that was the case, why had he just happily presided over a manslaughter conviction? It was Katz who took first-degree murder off the table in the first place. Detective Harold Johnston, one of the police officers involved in this case, later said he lost his faith in the justice system when Sweeney got off with a manslaughter rap. Judge Burton S. Katz was dubbed one of the worst judges in history at the end of this legal fiasco.

Upon his release from prison, John Sweeney changed his name and tried to resume his career as a chef. For many years though Dominique Dunne's family hired private detectives to keep track of Sweeney and made sure to let any new employers or friends (and especially girlfriends) he found know who he really was and what he had done to their precious daughter. It would not bring back Dominique but at the very least they were extracting some sort of revenge on Sweeney.

The most frustrating thing for the family of Dominique Dunne was that they had always been fearful of what John Sweeney might be capable of and were desperate for their daughter to extricate herself from the relationship. Sweeney had been violent with her in the past and was prone to explosive fits of jealousy. He once even threatened a fan who had innocently asked for Dominique's autograph. It is a great tragedy that she couldn't free herself of this vile man soon enough to prevent her sadly premature and senseless death.

Dominique's funeral was held on November 6, 1982 at The Good Shepherd Church in Beverly Hills. She was buried at Westwood Memorial Park.

Several years later her young Poltergeist co-star Heather O'Rourke would be buried there too.

PEG ENTWISTLE

Millicent Lilian "Peg" Entwistle was born on February the 5th, 1908, and grew up in Wales and London. She moved to the United States as a young woman and became a stage actress on Broadway. She was blonde haired and attractive (she looks a bit like Kirsten Dunst in some of her photos) and appeared on the stage with the likes of Ethel Barrymore and

Humphrey Bogart (who were obviously rising actors at the time and not yet famous). Peg Entwistle soon began to make waves on the stage and earned a lot of acclaim for her performances. No lesser figure than Bette Davis is said to have become a fan after watching Entwistle on the stage. Now that she had made her mark on the stage, Peg now targeted the next obvious rung up the ladder - movies. She dreamed of becoming a film star and appeared to have all the necessary attributes to do so.

Peg Entwistle landed her first (and sadly last) film role in a 1932 thriller called Thirteen Women. She was only in a supporting role but it was a break and foot in the door nonetheless. Peg had high hopes for the film and a movie career but she was dismayed when most of her supporting role in Thirteen Women ended up on the cutting room floor. Entwistle's role originally amounted to about twenty minutes of screen time (which was fairly major in an hour long film) but in the final version - after editing - Peg Entwistle was upset to see that she was only in the film for about four minutes.

The extensive cuts were made after the film scored low marks with preview audiences. Peg was pretty devastated because it seemed that preview audiences and the editor patently didn't want to see more of her character in the film. Her performance evidently hadn't made much of an impression at all. After the disappointing experience of Thirteen Women, Peg Entwistle found her dreams of Hollywood success had evaporated in swift and cruel fashion. She was offered no more film work and ran out of money. She couldn't even afford to get out of Hollywood and go back to New York where she'd enjoyed success on the stage. Peg felt friendless and alone. She felt like she had hit rock bottom.

Peg Entwistle decided to end her life. She did this in dramatic and bizarre fashion. Entwistle climbed up to the top of the famous Hollywood sign in the hills of Los Angeles and jumped from the letter H. She apparently used a ladder to get up there although where this ladder came from is something of a mystery. At the time the sign read Hollywoodland rather than Hollywood. It was all academic anyway. Peg was determined to jump and go out in the most theatrical way possible.

Why she chose such a bizarre death is open to question. It could be that Peg's less than subtle intended subtext was designed to declare that Hollywood had killed her by destroying her dreams. A hiker found her body. Peg had died as a result of multiple fractures from the fall. She was 24 years-old. It is possible that she may have been alive for some time after the fall and in agony. It definitely wasn't the most logical way to end it all. Peg left a suicide note which read - "I am afraid I am a coward. I am sorry for everything. If I had done this a long time ago it would have saved a lot of pain."

There was a rather tragic coda to her death because one day after her suicide, a letter was delivered to Peg's apartment from the Beverly Hills Playhouse offering her a part in a new play. Had this letter arrived one day earlier she probably wouldn't have killed herself. The death of Peg Entwistle earned big headlines in the media because of the theatrical and strange nature of her death. Given her desire to be a famous actress, it was darkly ironic that Peg became much more famous in death than she had been in life.

Trivia - Peg's ghost is said to haunt the area near the Hollywood sign. Several people have reported encountering it over the years.

CHRISTINA GRIMMIE

Christina Grimmie was a New Jersey born singer who first became famous and noticed after singing songs on YouTube. On the back of this she competed on the talent show The Voice (finishing in third place) and released an EP. Grimmie even launched an acting career by appearing in the 2016 independent film The Matchbreaker. She was famous for her high vocal range and an animal rights activist. Grimmie soon attracted famous friends and admirers and seemed like a very likeable and decent person. Christina Grimmie seemed set for a very promising career and even picked up a Teen Choice Award for her music. Fate was to intervene though in shocking fashion.

On June 10, 2016, Grimmie performed a show in Orlando and signed some autographs for fans in the arena after the concert. Grimmie was very generous in taking time out to talk to fans and sign autographs and she enjoyed this fan interaction because being famous was still relatively new to her and so it was all rather novel and flattering. She was just a nice person who was happy to meet new people and thank anyone who supported her music career by coming out to watch her sing and perform.

At one point during her autograph signing session, Grimmie innocently moved forward to hug a fan who appeared to be moving in for an autograph. At this moment, to the absolute horror of everyone, the fan produced a gun and shot her multiple times. The disturbed fan was a 27 year-old man named Kevin James Loibl. Grimmie's brother managed to wrestle Loibl to the ground but he then broke free and shot himself dead. Christina Grimmie's own injuries were - sadly -

fatal. She had been shot four times. A food vendor at the arena later said he heard four or five quick shots and saw Grimmie lying on the floor covered in blood. It was a horrifying scene.

Although she was taken to hospital Christina Grimmie was pronounced dead about thirty minutes after the fatal shooting took place. She was just twenty-two years-old. Kevin James Loibl had travelled to Orlando for the concert from his home in St. Petersburg, Florida. In his bag that night he had two guns, ammunition, and a hunting knife. The police believed he had developed a romantic obsession with Christina Grimmie and decided that if he couldn't have her then no one else would. The family of Loibl said they had no idea he was even a fan of Christina Grimmie - let alone had plans to kill her.

There was some criticism of the arena security that night because although they were supposed to search people going in the searches hadn't been that thorough because Loibl was able to walk in with two guns and a knife. In fairness to the staff they obviously could have no way of knowing that a disturbed fan was planning to kill Christina that night. What might have prevented the tragedy was metal detectors as people went in but sadly no such provision had been made that night. The arena staff obviously presumed that Christina's fans were harmless kids just out to have a good time - and all but one were. Thousands of fans attended the memorial service for Christina Grimmie. A bright young life had been wiped out in the most harrowing and unexpected fashion.

COREY HAIM

The Canadian actor Corey Haim was a big child/teen star in the mid to late 1980s. His films included The Lost Boys, Lucas, Watchers, and Silver Bullet. If you were a kid watching movies and renting VHS tapes in the mid to late eighties then you would definitely have been aware of Corey Haim. Haim was good looking (his trademark was his lopsided smirk) but could also be sympathetic and sensitive on the screen. He seemed to have a bit more depth and vulnerability than your average teen idol.

However, Haim found life in Hollywood much tougher when he got a few years older and started to age out of the teen roles that had made him famous and much in demand. As his cute kid looks began to fade thanks to the passage of time, drugs and his lifestyle, Haim's career fell off a cliff in the 1990s and he began appearing in straight to video movies. It was a far cry from the days when when he frequently graced the covers of teen magazines and was famous for his movie double-act with Corey Feldman.

Haim was addicted to drugs and ended up threatening his manager with a gun. He was then handed a past-due tax bill and sued by his insurance company for not disclosing his drug addiction. The money Haim had earned from his movies was soon all gone and he end up shuttling in and out of rehab. At one point Haim was homeless and reduced to trying to sell clumps of his hair on ebay. Corey Feldman claims that Haim was the victim of child sexual abuse in Hollywood and was sexually assaulted by Charlie Sheen while making the 1986 film Lucas. Charlie Sheen has dismissed these claims as nonsense.

On March 10, 2010, Corey Haim died at Providence Saint Joseph Medical Center of an apparent overdose. He was 38 years-old. A lot of people thought it was pretty shabby that Haim didn't feature in the 'In Memoriam' section of the Oscars when he died. It was a classic and sobering example of how you can be really famous in Hollywood for a time and then completely forgotten. Corey Haim was a huge star in the late 1980s but his fame and success was to be brief and troubled. Once his star faded he never managed to get his life back together and - like so many famous people who died young - paid a heavy price for his drug addictions.

Sadly, Hollywood history is full of child and teen stars like

Corey Haim who couldn't make a successful transition to adult life and success as a mature actor. Jake Lloyd played young Anakin Skywalker in the 1999 film Star Wars: Episode I – The Phantom Menace. Lloyd was only eight when cast. You might think this was a dream part but nothing could be farther from the truth. Lloyd and the film were both panned in reviews and he grew to hate Star Wars. He made two more films and then retired from acting. He was monosyllabic and sarcastic in interviews and clearly an unhappy and troubled young man.

In 2015, Lloyd was arrested for reckless driving, driving without a license, and resisting arrest. There were stories that he attacked his mother and that he was in an institution.

Mischa Barton first came to prominence at the age of eleven with an impressive performance in the cult film Lawn Dogs. She then had parts in Knotting Hill and The Sixth Sense and studied acting at The Royal Academy of Dramatic Art in London. A great career seemed to be ahead of Barton but she made a surprising move when she signed to be in the teen drama The OC in 2003.

After she left the show, Barton's acting career literally went nowhere fast. She was arrested for drink driving, was filmed having blazing arguments with her mother, ended up in hospital for drinking while on antibiotics, and was arrested for driving without a licence. Just to finish it all off, a sex tape featuring Barton surfaced in 2017 and she had to fight to stop its release. These days, Barton can be seen in bargain basement horror movies and reality shows. She is sad proof that a precocious child actor doesn't always become a successful actor when they grow-up.

Few people had such a steep and rapid decline as Edward Furlong - who was cast in Terminator 2 when he was fourteen. These days Furlong is a bloated and drug addled former star and a long way removed from the promising young actor he used to be in the early 1990s. Furlong confessed that by the age of 22 he was a cocaine and heroin abuser. He was also arrested for drunk driving and disorderly conduct. At a party he nearly died from an overdose and was found in his own vomit. When they made Terminator 3 in 2003 they gave Furlong a wide berth and cast Nick Stahl as John Connor instead (somewhat ironic as Nick Stahl later had his own problems with drink and drugs and was arrested more than once himself).

In 2009, Furlong's wife Rachael Bella filed a restraining order against him after he allegedly struck her and left threatening messages on the answerphone. When he appeared in court for violating the order, Furlong admitted he was broke and had no money. For several years he had been reduced to cheap direct to DVD horror films and comedies. His career, which had once been so promising, was all but dead.

He was later arrested for domestic abuse of Monica Keena, accused by his ex-wife of giving their six year-old son cocaine, and served six months in jail for violating probation. Furlong's looks were ravaged by drink and drugs. Today, bloated and bleary eyed, he is far removed from the fresh faced teenager who looked set for stardom in the early 1990s.

Martha Plimpton made her screen debut when she was eleven years-old. Years later she said that being a child star was something that came with obvious pitfalls. "When children's lives become all about external validation, that can set them up horribly. Because what's adorable when you're 12 isn't when you're 25. So when you wake up one day and realize the phone isn't ringing, what happens? You start thinking, 'How do I replicate that high?' And you do anything necessary to keep yourself in the spotlight. The second you put (younger people) in the spotlight, you've exploited them.

That's the very nature of show business, and sadly some are sacrificed to our need to watch, explore and enjoy - and Hollywood's need to make money."

PHIL HARTMAN

The Canadian born Phil Hartman was a comedian and actor best known for his work on The Simpsons and Saturday Night Live. His most famous sketch came when he played Bill Clinton visiting a McDonald's and eating everyone's food as he canvassed for votes. His many movie and TV roles included Pee-wee's Big Adventure, Three Amigos!, and The Larry Sanders Show. Hartman was popular and fairly low-key away from the screen. He seemed quite a private person and was said to be difficult to get to know because he always stayed in character and never revealed his real self. Hartman was described as a team player by those who worked with him. He had no desire for leading roles or the limelight. Hartman was happy to be a supporting character actor. He was always much in demand for voice work too.

Hartman's third wife was a woman named Brynn Omdahl. Omdahl had drug addictions which she battled with all the time. She also had a history of depression. The relationship between the couple was what you might describe as obstreperous at times. They would argue and fight now and again but then many couples do. In this particular case though the arguments would led to tragedy. On the evening of May 27, 1998, the couple had a heated argument. Hartman went to bed alone and his wife stormed off. Hours later, Omdahl returned to their house at 3 am to find Hartman asleep in bed. She took out a handgun and shot him three times - two of the bullets were fired at his head and one at his side.

Hartman had no chance of surviving the shooting at such close range. He was forty-nine years-old. Omdahl had been using cocaine and drinking and was both high and intoxicated. She drove to the house of a friend to confess to the murder and they then returned to the house where Hartman had been shot. When the friend saw the evidence for himself he called the police. While they waited for the police to arrive, Omdahl locked herself in the bathroom and then committed suicide by shooting herself. The bullet wound went through one of her eyes.

Although friends and neighbours say they had detected some tension in the marriage, no one suspected that Omdahl was capable of killing her husband. The fact that she was intoxicated at the time and barely knew what she was doing made it all the more senseless and tragic. What was especially sad about this case is that the couple had two children but now they would have to grow up with no parents. The children, Birgen Anika Hartman and Sean Edward Hartman, then nine and six years old, eventually moved into the home of their maternal aunt and her husband. Their names were changed to give them privacy and by all accounts they are doing fine now and successful and happy adults.

JON ERIK HEXUM

Jon-Erik Hexum was an American model and actor. His beefy good looks soon attracted the attention of casting agents and in 1982 he was cast as the lead in the NBC time travel show Voyagers. Voyagers was a goofy but entertaining piece of nonsense in which Hexum played an intrepid adventurer. The show brought Hexum to the attention of Joan Collins - who cast him in the 1983 TV movie The Making of a Male Model. In 1983 Hexum was cast in the CBS show Cover Up. In the show Hexum played a special forces operative who helps a woman (played by Jennifer O'Neill) find the people who killed her husband. The cover for the special operative was to pose as a male model.

Hexum, still in his mid-twenties, was seen as someone who could potentially become a big star in Hollywood. It seemed more than likely that he would break free of television (which in the 1980s didn't have the prestige it enjoys today - today television has equal status with film) and do movies. Hexum made his film debut as quarterback Pat Trammell in the Bear

Bryant biopic The Bear with Gary Busey. Hexum was a football player as a teenager and at 6'1 and 200 pounds was perfectly convincing as an athlete. He was pretty good in The Bear and showed he was capable of doing other things besides action roles and playing male model types.

Hexum was the sort of actor who would get an audition when they were casting James Bond purely for his looks alone. Sadly though, Hexum was to meet a bizarre and tragic end. On Friday, October 12, 1984, Hexum was on the set of Cover Up and waiting around to shoot a scene. Bored with the delays he started goofing around with a prop magnum handgun which was loaded with blank cartridges. Hexum had presumed the gun was completely harmless and fake but this wasn't quite the case.

He started pretending to play Russian roulette and put the gun to his head and pulled the trigger as a joke. The blank gun though was filled with paper wadding and at close range some of this wadding entered Hexum's skull and caused massive haemorrhaging in his brain. The impact from the blast fractured his skull and drive a piece of bone into his brain. Jon-Erik Hexum was taken to hospital but declared brain dead a week later and taken off life support. He was just 26 years-old.

Hexum's character in Cover Up was replaced by a new character played by Anthony Hamilton (who was equally doomed and died of AIDs) and the show limped on for a short while afterwards before being cancelled due to poor ratings. The family of Hexum won an undisclosed compensation settlement with Twentieth Century Fox Television and Glenn Larson Productions over his death. It was a strange and tragic accident but - clearly - safety on the set could have been better. Not only was the prop gun dangerous but surely someone on the set should have told Hexum not to fool around with it?

The only happy note to this sad story is that Hexum's organs were donated by his family after his death and saved lives.

Despite his beefcake image, Hexum had a university degree and played the piano. He was intelligent and ambitious. Sadly, we'll never know now what he might have gone on to accomplish.

THOMAS INCE

Thomas Ince was a highly influential and innovative figure in the early development of the motion picture industry in Hollywood. He was also one of those Old Hollywood figures who died in mysterious circumstances. Ince was one of the first tycoons in the film industry and is credited with creating the first movie studio. The company he created eventually became known as MGM. After he sold MGM he went on to create Paramount Pictures and then started a new studio after selling up.

In 1924, Ince went on a yacht cruise which included a number of famous guests like Charlie Chaplin. After he began to feel poorly after dinner, Ince was taken from the yacht to a hospital in Los Angeles. A day after the hospital he died at the age of 44. The official cause of death was cited as heart failure. However, there is plenty of Old Hollywood gossip about this sudden and unexpected death. Legend has it that William Randolph Hearst, the famous businessman who owned the yacht, had found Charlie Chaplin seducing his mistress Marion Davies (who was an actress and also obviously on the yacht) and tried to shoot Chaplin. The bullet missed and killed Ince.

The theory goes that Hearst used his power and influence to cover the whole thing up and make it look as if Ince had died of natural causes. The evidence for this theory? Well, Ince was cremated very quickly and his widow had a trust fund set up by a mysterious benefactor. It is also said that a witness to the shooting was given a lucrative employment contract by Hearst to ensure his silence. It could be that Thomas Ince really did die of natural causes but it appears there is still enough mystery concerning his demise to provide sufficient room for a few dark theories.

MICHAEL JACKSON

Michael Jackson was born in 1958 in Gary, Indiana. He had five brothers (Jackie, Tito, Jermaine, Marlon, and Randy) and three sisters (Rebbie, La Toya, and Janet). The Jacksons grew up in a musical family as their parents were both musicians and loved singing. The family patriarch Joe Jackson was said to be a hard taskmaster. He was strict and wanted discipline from his children. The children developed obvious musical talents at a young age - especially Michael. He could sing and dance almost as soon as he could walk. Michael and his brothers formed a band known as the Jackson 5. They played in bars and clubs and signed a record deal with Motown Records. They had a number one album and hit singles and Michael soon became very famous.

In the late 1970s, Michael Jackson went solo and after some early struggles his 1982 album Thriller made him one of the biggest stars in the world. The title song had a fantastic horror themed music video directed by John Landis. Michael Jackson would release further albums in the years to come and they were usually much anticipated. His stage shows were much in demand too and he had a loyal army of worldwide fans. It soon became evident though in private (and indeed public) that Michael Jackson was a rather odd character to say the least. He lived on a ranch that had been turned into a theme park and his closest friends always seemed to be children - specifically young boys and male teenagers.

Michael Jackson's appearance changed drastically over the years too because of endless plastic surgery. His skin also became progressively lighter (his doctor said Jackson suffered from the pigmentation disease vitiligo). Why Michael Jackson felt the need to change his appearance so much is open to speculation. He simply didn't seem comfortable in his own skin. Jackson looked rather freakish in the end because of all the surgery. He was also a shy and famously eccentric man.

Jackson was married twice. His first marriage was to Lisa Marie Presley, daughter of the famous rock singer Elvis Presley. His second marriage was to a nursing assistant named Debbie Rowe - with whom he had two children. These marriages, whether fairly or unfairly, were looked upon with some degree of scepticism. Many felt the first was a charade designed to mitigate rumours (and eventual court cases) that Jackson had sexually abused boys and that the second marriage was simply arranged to produce children by artificial means.

Michael Jackson stood trial for child abuse allegations while he was alive but somehow managed to avoid punishment. The trial became a bizarre spectacle in the end - especially when Jackson turned up to court one day in his pyjamas. Jackson seemed increasingly frail during the trial and could barely seem to stand up at times. He was clearly not looking after himself very well. Jackson died in 2009 at the age of fifty. At the time he was preparing for a comeback concert in London which had been forced upon him because of financial trouble. In reality he was in no fit state to go back on the stage.

Jackson's doctor had prescribed him powerful medication (used on horses!) to help him sleep and this had caused a heart attack. A quack doctor indeed. The world was shocked by the death of Michael Jackson because he was so talented and had so many fans. It's always strange when someone mega famous dies because we have this weird childlike sense that fame somehow protects one from ordinary and unwelcome things - like death!- but of course it doesn't. Celebrities are just flesh and blood like the rest of us. Jackson liked to compare himself to Peter Pan and believed he would never die. He had fallen so far down the rabbit hole of fantasy he had completely lost touch with reality.

Jackson's legacy was tarnished in death (as it had been in life) by further allegations that he had sexually abused boys on his Neverland ranch. Jackson fans simply refused to believe the allegations though and prefer to remember him as an iconic entertainer. There is no doubt that in the 80s and 90s Michael Jackson was the biggest star in show business.

ANISSA JONES

Anissa Jones became famous as the blonde haired kid Buffy on the sitcom Family Affair. The show ran on CBS from 1966 to 1971. Annissa Jones was a charismatic and talented child actor and seemed to have a bright future ahead of her. She even made an amusing appearance as a guest on Dick Cavett's chat show and also appeared as guest on Rowan & Martin's Laugh-In. Jones was considered to be a kind and generous kid and was popular with the cast and crew of Family Affair. Anissa Jones was thirteen when Family Affair ended and, like many child actors, found that life after appearing in a successful TV show was difficult.

The only acting credit of Jones apart from Family Affair turned out to be in an episode of a short-lived 1970 sitcom called To Rome With Love. She actually tested for the part played by Linda Blair in The Exorcist but the director William Friedkin felt that Jones was too associated with Family Affair to be believable in a different role. Jones was dismayed by the fact that she already seemed to be typecast and so drifted away from acting. The fact she she was only 4'11, even as a growing teenager, was also likely to limit what parts she could play. It must have been pretty weird for Anissa to realise she was washed-up in Hollywood at the tender age of thirteen.

While there are many cases of child actors successfully making the transition to adult roles (one thinks of people like Christian Bale, Jodi Foster, Joseph Gordon-Levitt etc), Anissa Jones seemed unlikely to be one of them. She was typecast as a little wisecracking kid with pigtails but this was the type of part she was too old to play now. It is said though that Anissa Jones had no great interest in fame for the sake of fame and just wanted to be an ordinary person. After spending much of her childhood in a television studio she came to feel that leaving the world of showbusiness behind wouldn't be so bad.

However, ordinary life didn't turn out to be as easy or satisfying as she had suspected. She began to go off the rails and exhibit worrying behaviour. Anissa began to shoplift and even worked in a Donut store to make ends meet. When she turned eighteen, Anissa came into possession of the trust fund money that she had earned on Family Affair. This turned out to be a recipe for disaster as Anissa had developed drug habits and addictions by now. The trust fund money meant that Anissa now had plenty of money to buy drugs and booze. In many ways getting that money was the worst thing that could have happened.

In August 1976, Anissa Jones died after taking a cocktail of barbiturates, phencyclidine, cocaine and methaquaalone. An unidentified blue liquid was also found with her drugs stash. She was just eighteen years-old. Her death was apparently not a suicide or overdose. Anissa had apparently just lost track of how many drugs she had taken that fateful day. Friends had found her unresponsive in bed and despite extensive resuscitation efforts by paramedics she tragically died.

After her death, Annissa's doctor was charged for illegally prescribing her Seconal. Secobarbital is a short-acting barbiturate derivative drug. It possesses anaesthetic, anticonvulsant, anxiolytic, sedative, and hypnotic properties. As for why Anissa Jones went off the rails so rapidly and tragically, the general theory seems to be that her rebellious streak and drugs problems only became apparent after the death of her father. Anissa lived with her father after her parents got divorced so she obviously took this loss very badly. All in all this was a very sad and tragic story - especially for those who had grown up watching Family Affair.

ROB KNOX

Rob Knox was a young English actor who was born in Kent in 1989. His first credited role was in the ITV police show The Bill and he also had an uncredited part in the 2004 Clive Owen film King Arthur. He had a huge break in 2008 when he was cast as Marcus Belby in the movie Harry Potter and the Half-Blood Prince. Knox had also signed to appear in the next movie - Harry Potter and the Deathly Hallows (which was eventually split into two parts). Knox must have been pretty excited at the thought of the career options and money that might come his way out of the Harry Potter association. Fate was to intervene in heartless fashion though.

On 24 May 2008, Rob Knox was in his home town of Sidcup and during a night out intervened to protect his brother from a man who was threatening him with two knives. The man was twenty-two year-old Karl Bishop. A few weeks earlier, Bishop had apparently had an altercation with Knox and accused him of stealing a phone (which he hadn't). Karl Bishop was basically a lunatic with no moral compass. He was a wild and feral character and a sociopath. Sociopaths lack a sense of responsibility or a social conscience. They are prone to antisocial behaviour. They can then tilt into becoming a psychopath. A psychopath has even less of a moral compass than a sociopath. Sociopaths do not have a rational and logical voice in their head telling them that a course of action is wrong. They will ignore and banish any such thoughts. They have no empathy, thought, or remorse for their victims.

The tragic night in question, Knox had rugby tackled Bishop to protect his brother Jamie. Bishop then stabbed Knox in the buttock and four times in the chest. The fatal blow apparently came when Bishop - who was clearly completely crazy - stabbed Knox in the head. Others who tried to intervene were also stabbed by Bishop - one receiving spinal injuries and another knife wounds to the face. The friends of Rob Knox were very brave that night because, at great risk to themselves, they eventually managed to restrain Bishop long enough for the police to arrive. Sadly though, the injuries to Rob Knox were so severe he died. Knox was just eighteen years-old.

Karl Bishop was sentenced to life for the murder of Rob Knox. He showed no remorse in court and smirked and smiled during the trial. He was a truly vile and despicable person with no compassion or humanity at all. Bishop was one of those people where you really hope he never gets out of prison. They should just throw away the key and forget about him. It transpired that Bishop always carried knives and had been wanted in connection with a robbery he conducted at knifepoint. It wasn't much consolation to the family of Rob Knox but at least this dangerous and awful young man was behind bars and no longer a danger to society.

The heartbroken family of Rob Knox said that it was typical of his character that he had sacrificed his life trying to protect others. His death prompted the British government to announce new measures cracking down on knife crimes and the possession of these dangerous weapons. Sadly though, knife crime is a problem that seems to never go away. Why anyone would go out carrying knives (let alone use them to hurt people) is a baffling mystery to most normal people but - alas - it still seems to happen.

KATERINA Z KOMAROVA

Kateřina z Komárova, whose birth date is uncertain, was a Czech noblewoman who became an infamous figure for the mistreatment on servants and serfs on her estate. She was convicted for fourteen murders but might have killed as many as thirty people. Komárova was married to Jan Bechyně - who was quite a big cheese when it came to power and politics. He was essentially a count and had judicial, political, and military power over a large region.

Because of his duties, Jan Bechyně spent a lot of time away from the family estate and this was bad news for the servants because they were left at the mercy of Kateřina z Komárova. She was said to have tortured her servants by means of cruel punishments that left many of them dead. If you only committed a minor transgression on the estate you were still given a horrendously harsh punishment. Komárova would cut people with knives and put salt in the wounds. It is said that she poured boiling hot butter over some servants as a punishment. Servants had both boiling hot water and ice cold water thrown over them as punishment.

Stories of Komárova's brutal treatment of the servants eventually began to abound in the region and a local Dean got involved in the case. However, Komárova's husband threatened to sue the Dean for even daring to suggest that his wife had been responsible for such awful things. Eventually a trial of sorts was arranged for the servants to tell their side of the story but they were so terrified of Komárova they refused at first to speak of her crimes.

It took one brave serf to speak up though and pretty soon they were all coming forward with tales about the cruelty of Komárova. She eventually confessed to killing fourteen serfs but the true figure was almost certainly higher than that. Komárova didn't seem to express any remorse for her crimes or ever give the impression that she felt she had done anything wrong. As a punishment she was thrown into the Mihulka tower at Prague Castle to starve to death. This happened in around two weeks.

VERONICA LAKE

Veronica Lake was one of the most iconic stars in Hollywood history and famed for her 1940s femme fatale roles. Though she was pretty short, Lake looked like a million dollars on the screen and was much in demand. She was best known for her peek-a-boo hairstyle - which women of the era frequently tried to imitate. You think that Jennifer Anniston's haircut in Friends was famous? Veronica Lake's hair was a million times more famous in her era. Trivia - the American government complained about American women copying Lake's hairstyle because long hair was dangerous in the machinery festooned factories where many women worked during World War 2. Lake actually changed her hair as a consequence and this might actually have damaged her acting career.

Lake's career eventually began to slowly fizzle out after World War 2. She appeared in a few films which turned out to be stinkers and she began to drink too much. In the end she lost her contracts with the big film studios. Her later life was difficult and even tragic. She battled schizophrenia and alcoholism and barely acted again after 1952. In the 1960s, Lake worked as a waitress in a hotel and booze took a heavy toll on her famous looks. She made a return to acting in the trashy bargain basement horror film Flesh Feast in 1970. Lake appears drunk in the film and doesn't seem to have any teeth. This was a rather sad epilogue to one of the most famous careers in Hollywood.

Lake died of acute renal failure in 1973 at the age of 50. The doctors and nurses at the hospital were amazed that Veronica Lake never seemed to have any visitors. It felt like this legendary star had been completely forgotten. Though she was married three times and had four children she seemed to be estranged from all of them. Lake's ashes remained in a funeral home for three years because no one wanted to pay any expenses.

Thankfully, her sad end hasn't diminished what she accomplished when she was alive. Lake now has a Hollywood star and is regarded to be one of the most iconic leading ladies in Hollywood history.

MICHAEL LANDON

Michael Landon was a beloved television actor who became like a one man industry in the end. He made his film debut in 1957 in the film I Was A Teenage Werewolf but then became really famous when he played Little Joe on the television show Bonanza. Bonanza was hugely popular and Landon was in the show for fourteen years. You'd think that Bonanza would be a hard act to follow but Landon then had an equally famous show with Little House on the Prairie - an adaptation of Laura Ingalls Wilder's best-selling series of Little House books. Landon played Charles Ingalls in the show and directed many of the episodes.

Little House on the Prairie ran from 1974 to 1983 and was hugely popular. Landon was very hands-on with the show and something of a workaholic. You could say that Landon's shows were a trifle schmaltzy and old-fashioned but he felt television was rather cynical at times and liked to create shows with a moral compass that the whole family could watch. Landon made a couple of films in the early eighties (Love Is Forever, Sam's Son) but one of these premiered on television anyway. Television was his home and where he belonged.

After the end of Little House on the Prairie in 1983, Landon wasted no time in creating another TV show for himself. Highway to Heaven began in 1984 and starred Landon as Jonathan Smith, an angel who is sent to Earth to do good deeds. In the show Landon teamed up with his friend and Prairie co-star Victor French (who played a former police officer named Mark Gordon who travels around with Smith helping people in need). Landon's new show was dubbed Jesus in Malibu by cynics and it was even more sentimental than Little House on the Prairie but it was good wholesome family fun.

Landon would star in and direct Highway to Heaven during the week and then edit the episodes at the weekend. Trivia -

one of the guest stars on Heaven was a child actor named Paul Walker. Highway to Heaven didn't have the legs of Prairie though and was cancelled after five seasons when it began to slide in the ratings. Landon suffered a personal blow too when Victor French died of cancer shortly after completing the fifth season of Highway to Heaven.

Landon, never one to sit on his thumbs, then began planning a new television show called Us. A two hour pilot for the show was shot (which Landon naturally wrote and directed). In the new show Landon was to play a man wrongfully convicted of murder. After he is declared innocent, Landon's character (who has spent eighteen years in prison) reconnects with his father and son as they travel around the United States helping people. It was a very Michael Landon sort of scenario for a television show and probably would have been very watchable and sweet. Sadly though, Landon didn't live to make Us. He died before the pilot had even aired.

In early 1991, Landon began to feel unwell during a family vacation. He decided to go to hospital and have some tests. He presumed he might have an ulcer but it turned out to be much worse than that. Landon had an aggressive form of pancreatic cancer which was inoperable. He was given only a 5% chance of survival. Landon went home to his house in Malibu and began chemotherapy. He also sought out alternative remedies. He took up a vegetarian diet and had coffee enemas to relieve the pain of his treatment. Although Landon said he was going to do his best to beat the disease the odds were against him.

In May 1991 he made his final public appearance when he appeared on The Johnny Carson Show. Landon was funny and in good spirits that night but in reality he only had weeks to live. On July 1, 1991, at age 54, Michael Landon died. He died only three months after first learning that he had cancer. Landon blamed his cancer on the fact that he had been a chainsmoker for much of his life and also ate the wrong things. There could be another explanation though.

Little House on the Prairie was shot on land purchased in Simi Valley Ranch. The land came at a bargain price because an experimental sodium cooled nuclear reactor operated by the Rocketdyne Corporation had once released a huge wave of radioactivity in the area. Although the land was deemed safe to shoot Little House on the Prairie, it is open to question as to whether or not this was actually the case. Five members of the cast later died from cancer - most famously Michael Landon. Patrick Swayze, who had connections to Simi Valley, also died of pancreatic cancer at a fairly young age.

This was not the first time something like this may have happened. The 1956 John Wayne film The Conqueror was shot in Utah near an area where nuclear weapons testing had taken place in the 1950s. The director Dick Powell died of cancer several years later and the two lead actors John Wayne and Pedro Armendáriz also developed cancer. Nearly half of the cast and crew later developed cancer and nearly fifty of them died. It is unavoidably speculated then that the cast and crew were working in an area that still had dangerous traces of radiation fallout.

BRANDON LEE

Brandon Lee was the handsome son of the legendary Bruce Lee and began a promising career in Hollywood with action roles. Brandon's movies (Legacy of Rage, Laser Mission, Showdown in Little Tokyo, Rapid Fire) hadn't got great reviews but the critics were quite kind to him and said he was charismatic and likeable onscreen and had a good future in Hollywood. 1992's Rapid Fire was sort of like the first undiluted Brandon Lee film and suggested he could follow in the footsteps of people like Steven Seagal and Chuck Norris. Lee had an advantage over them too in that he looked a bit like Johnny Depp and was much younger.

Brandon signed on next to appear in a film called The Crow -

which was something of a departure. The Crow was a superhero film with horror elements and was considerably more ambitious than any film Brandon had been in before. Sadly, this would turn out to be Brandon's last film. He was killed shooting The Crow when a live primer in a dummy round hit him at point blank range during a gun sequence. He was only 28 years-old. The tragic accident happened on March 31, 1993. There were only eight days left on filming on the movie and Brandon was due to get married in the following few weeks when production on The Crow had concluded.

The actor Michael Masse, who played a villain in The Crow, was part of a scene in which his character shot Brandon's character. When the stunt was concluded the crew became aware that Brandon was not moving. There was now a hole in his abdomen and he was rushed to hospital. Despite six hours of surgery he died of his injuries. The accident had occurred because the bullets used in the gun had been converted to blanks from live bullets. Blanks are supposed to have cardboard tips so that in the event of any accidental contact the damage is minimal.

In this case though one of the lead tips from the modified live bullets was still in the gun and came loose during the scene - fatally hitting Brandon in the stomach. It was basically incompetence on the part of the people making the film. The death was ruled an accident but Brandon's mother Linda Lee Cadwell launched a civil suit against the film studio - which was eventually settled out of court. The Crow turned out to be a pretty good film but this was obviously scant consolation to the late Brandon Lee and his distraught family. The Crow might well have made Brandon Lee a big star had he lived but - alas - we'll never know how his career would panned out now.

The Crow was completed with the use of a double after Brandon's death. This was a rather spooky echo of how Bruce Lee's last film (Game of Death) was completed with a double after Bruce Lee died. It is sometimes said that Brandon fell victim to a family curse but this is patently fiction. The Crow was apparently quite an incompetent production and - sadly - it was safety issues on the set which cost Brandon Lee his life.

BRUCE LEE

Martial arts star Bruce Lee died at the age of 32 in July 1973. His death was completely unexpected and came as a great shock to the people of Hong Kong and China because he was more or less a superhero to them after appearing in local films like The Way of the Dragon and the Big Boss. Lee was not a star in America at the time because Enter the Dragon, the film that did make him a global star, was still a month from release at the time. it's a great shame that Bruce Lee didn't live to see the huge success of Enter the Dragon and Hollywood would surely have beckoned if he hadn't passed away in such unexpected fashion.

But what caused Bruce Lee's sudden death? How could someone who appeared to be so fit and healthy die so suddenly? The most common explanation for his death is that he died after an allergic reaction to aspirin. His death occurred after he visited the actress Betty Ting Pe in her apartment. Lee was having an affair with Betty Ting Pe - although this fact was covered up at the time lest it should damage Lee's reputation (he was married afterall). After he complained of a headache, Betty Ting Pe gave Lee an Equagesic - a common painkiller containing aspirin and a tranquilizer known as meprobamate.

Equagesic was felt to be harmless although it was discontinued in the United States after Lee's death. After taking the medicine, Lee had a lie down and never woke up. Though an ambulance was called and there were attempts to revive him he was pronounced dead in hospital. The coroner officially ruled Bruce Lee’s death the result of a second cerebral edema (this was not the first time Lee had suffered this condition) brought on by taking Equagesic.

Naturally, as no famous person can seem to die young without conspiracy theories abounding, there were plenty of these when Bruce Lee passed away. There were stories that he was killed by an organised crime group or had been the victim of a family curse (this theory is probably retrospective due to his son Brandon also tragically dying at a young age). A later theory (which doesn't seem implausible) is that Lee died of heatstroke after having sweat glands in his arm pits removed (Lee apparently hated the appearance of sweat on clothes). The day Lee died was ferociously hot in Hong Kong.

When it became public knowledge in Hong Kong that Lee had been with Betty Ting Pe when he died there were even theories that Betty Ting Pe had murdered him with poison. These theories were nonsense but Betty Ting Pe said she received death threats as a result of the gossip. Chuck Norris, who knew Bruce Lee and worked with him, suggested that muscle relaxants Lee took might have killed him. There are a lot of stories too that Bruce Lee, despite his monastic image, took a lot of recreational drugs and that these might have contributed to his demise. The death of Bruce Lee still remains something of a mystery after all these years but it appears that it was probably a natural medical demise rather than a conspiracy, murder, or outlandish supernatural curse.

JOHN LENNON

The music icon John Lennon was killed at the age of 40 by a disturbed fan named Mark Chapman. Chapman was a security guard with (no surprise here) mental health issues. He had contemplated suicide and become obsessed with John Lennon. He thought Lennon was a big old hypocrite for singing songs about money not being important despite being a millionaire who lived a lavish lifestyle. Chapman bought a gun and flew to New York where Lennon lived with Yoko Ono. He staked out the Dakota Apartments building where Lennon resided and would often sign autographs outside as he came and went from the building. Chapman even got Lennon's autograph himself before he returned to kill the music icon. Chapman later said that Lennon had been very nice and polite when he signed the autograph. That didn't stop him from shooting Lennon dead though.

When Yoko Ono and John Lennon returned to the Dakota at 10.50 pm, on Monday 8th December 1980, Chapman was waiting shot Lennon four times in the back. Less than half an hour later, Lennon was pronounced dead at the Roosevelt Hospital. Chapman did not flee the scene. He was detained by the Dakota's doorman until the police arrived. According to the autopsy report, two bullets entered the left side of Lennon's back, travelling through the left side of his chest and his left lung with one exiting from the body and one lodged in his neck. Two more bullets hit Lennon in his left shoulder. The chances of surviving these injuries were remote to say the least.

After he shot Lennon, Chapman apparently pulled out a copy of Thc Catcher in the Rye and started reading it. Inside his copy of The Catcher in the Rye, Chapman had written - "This is my statement", signing it "Holden Caulfield." Chapman was clearly a disturbed man. He had come to identify with Holden and viewed the world as being full of phonies. He claimed that he acted to preserve the 'innocence' of Lennon (which seems like a rather odd thing to say about a middle-aged millionaire musician who had known worldwide fame since the 1960s). Chapman felt Lennon had become a phoney. It came out during the court case that before the assassination Chapman would sit in his room chanting the mantra, “THE PHONY MUST DIE SAYS THE CATCHER IN THE RYE!”

Chapman changed his plea to guilty during the court case. His legal team had instructed him to enter a plea of not guilty by reason of insanity. The judge ordered psychiatric treatment for Chapman during his incarceration and sentenced him to twenty-years-to-life - five years less than the maximum sentence of twenty-five-years-to-life. Chapman has been denied parole eleven times and remains incarcerated in Wende Correctional Facility, east of Buffalo, New York. He has said that he regrets shooting John Lennon and shouldn't have done it but it's all a bit late now.

Another (and in this case attempted killer rather than actual murderer) disturbed individual who was linked to The Catcher in the Rye in the press was John Hinckley Jr. In the 1970s Hinckley developed an unhealthy obsession with the teenage actress Jodie Foster after she played an underage prostitute in the famous Martin Scorsese film Taxi Driver. Hinckley made repeated (and predictably unsuccessful) attempts to contact Foster and became so frustrated by his inability to make her take any notice of him that he decided to assassinate Ronald Reagan in mimicry of the alienated vigilante Travis Bickle in Taxi Driver.

Hinckley, completely detached from reality, thought this murder would impress Foster and that the actress would finally notice him. Reagan survived the 1981 bullet and Hinckley was found not guilty by reason of insanity and remained under institutional psychiatric care until September 2016 (on July 27, 2016, a federal judge ruled that Hinckley would be allowed to be released as he was no longer considered a threat to himself or others - the pivotal conditions of his release are that he has no contact with the Reagan family or Jodie Foster or Foster's family or agent). Hinckley was found to have a copy of The Catcher in the Rye among ten books the FBI found in his hotel room. There was also a book about John Lennon.

Another harrowing case sometimes connected with The Catcher in the Rye concerns Robert John Bardo. On July 18, 1989, Bardo murdered the actress Rebecca Schaeffer. Schaeffer was best known for her role in the sitcom My Sister Sam. We'll discuss this murder later in the book. After he shot Schaeffer, Bardo apparently left a copy of The Catcher in the Rye near the crime scene. It seems somewhat unfair for The Catcher in the Rye to be tarnished by these (thankfully) very few violent and sad events. Millions of people have read Salinger's novel. They haven't been turned into killers or would be Travis Bickles.

Mark Chapman was said to be fixated on the film Ordinary People. Hinckley had other books in his hotel room besides The Catcher in the Rye. Bardo, as his trial established, was more influenced by the U2 song 'Exit' than The Catcher in the Rye. The song was played in court as evidence and U2 stopped performing it for many years after Bardo cited it as an influence. These men were clearly all unstable and troubled. They would still have been unstable even in a world where The Catcher in the Rye didn't exist.

MARQUISE DE BRINVILLIERS

Marie-Madeleine d'Aubray - Marquise de Brinvilliers was born in Paris in 1630. She was a French aristocrat who murdered her father and brothers in order to inherit their estates. However, it is often claimed that killed dozens of people in hospitals while testing and refining the poison which she would used to kill her relatives. The truth of this later claim is disputed but it wouldn't surprise you if it was true. Marquise de Brinvilliers was clearly a ruthless and ambitious woman who would stop at nothing to get what she wanted. You can't imagine she was the sort of person who would lose much sleep over some people in hospital getting poisoned!

The Marquise was the eldest of the children in her family but she was not in line to inherit the estate. As a woman she was expected to marry into wealth and not burden the family. She had marriages and children but the Marquise was very promiscuous and had many lovers. This is said to have rankled her father because he felt she was risking shame on the family reputation. The Marquise's father was very angry when he learned that his daughter was having an affair with a man named Godin de Sainte-Croix so he arranged for Sainte-Croix to be arrested. It is naturally speculated that this action made the Marquise angry enough to contemplate murdering her father.

Godin de Sainte-Croix started an alchemy business when he was released from prison. He remained in (clandestine you would imagine) contact with the Marquise and through Sainte-Croix she learned a great deal about chemicals and poisons. It is claimed that the Marquise now conducted a number of experiments with poison on a local hospital in Paris and also on her own servants. Up to thirty people are alleged to have died as a result of these experiments. The source for this claim is a police report although, as we have noted, not everyone believes this happened. One can certainly build a case for it though.

Noble French figures were often expected to visit hospitals and the Marquise would have had ample opportunity to poison patients. Suspicious deaths in hospitals at the time would hardly have been noticed or logged in the 1660s in the way they would today. People simply died a lot more often in those days than they do today. Medical treatment was primitive and disease was more rampant. The Marquise could have offed a number of patients and servants for all we know.

In 1666 she began to poison her father. The Marquise actually put an employee of hers in the family home to finish her father off with poison. Her father, shortly before his death, invited her home and so she actually finished him off herself in the end. The Marquise then set about poisoning her brothers. This was a lot more difficult because she wasn't on good terms with them and they barely spoke to her. They did though live in the family home so she got a footman employed by the family to help her. One of the brothers was poisoned with an apple pie and they managed to get to the other brother too in the end.

Strangely, the Marquise seemed to get away with the murders at first despite the fact that they were highly suspicious. She was rumbled though when Godin de Sainte-Croix died. He was found to have letters in his possession from the Marquise in which she'd promised him a sum of money after the deaths of her father and brothers had been completed. Case closed. The participation of La Chaussée, the footman who helped in the murders, was also deduced and he fled. When he was captured, La Chaussée admitted that the Marquise had been behind the deaths of her relatives. The Marquise went on the run and tried to hide in England. She was eventually arrested in Belgium.

The Marquise at first denied all knowledge of the murders and said she had nothing to do with them. She said that Godin de Sainte-Croix must have killed them. However, she was not believed and sentenced to death. The Marquise was subject to a torture known as water cure before her death. In this rather unpleasant practice the victim is forced to drink large quantities of water in a short time until their stomach is full and they can barely breathe. The Marquise was then beheaded with a sword in 1676. She was 45 years-old.

SAL MINEO

Sal Mineo was an actor best remembered for playing John "Plato" Crawford opposite James Dean in the film Rebel Without a Cause. Mineo was twice nominated for the Academy Award for Best Supporting Actor for his roles in Rebel Without a Cause and Exodus. Sal Mineo was a big teen idol in his day and was deluged with fan letters. His career though seemed to fade much faster than anticipated. This is generally felt to have been a consequence of the fact that it was an open secret that Mineo was bisexual and didn't care if anyone knew about it. These days no cares cares about the sexuality of actors but it was - sadly - a different matter in Mineo's day. His sexuality is alleged to have cost him parts in the end.

The sexuality of actors in Hollywood was once a very big deal to studios. They even had what were known as lavender marriages. Lavender marriages were a facet of Old Hollywood that seem preposterous today. A lavender marriage was where it would be arranged by the studio for a gay actor to marry a member of the opposite sex to quash rumours about their sexuality. The most famous example of this is Rock Hudson, who was gay in real life, marrying his secretary Phyllis Gates. It is often speculated that Danny Kaye's marriage to Sylvia Fine was a lavender marriage and it has been said that Barbara Stanwyck and Robert Taylor married each other to BOTH quash rumours about their sexuality.

Not everyone was willing to go along with Hollywood's attempt to mask the private lives of the stars. William Haines, who is often referred to as Hollywood's first openly gay actor, ignored pressure from studios to enter in a lavender marriage in the 1930s and saw his career come to an abrupt halt as a consequence. Haines opened up an interior design business and got out of acting altogether because he refused to lie about who he really was. Sal Mineo was cut from the same cloth as Haines. He didn't care if people knew about his sexuality.

Mineo was said to be rather baffled when the film roles began to dry up. He auditioned to be in big films like The Godfather but obviously didn't get cast. After a part in Escape from the Planet of the Apes he drifted into television and appeared in shows like Columbo and Hawaii Five-O. Sal Mineo did stage a theatre comeback though and won rave reviews for his work on the stage. This might well have led to a film renaissance had he lived.

Sadly though, on February 12, 1976, Mineo was stabbed to death in the alley behind his West Hollywood apartment building. Sal was returning home at about 11-30 at night after doing some rehearsals for a play he was appearing in. He had just parked his car in the garage when a man with a knife appeared and confronted him. People nearby heard screams and found Sal lying in a pool of blood. The blade had pierced his heart.

Because his wallet was still on him the police ruled out robbery as a motive at first. This was pretty odd because a man was seen running from the scene. It seemed pretty obvious that the man hadn't had time to search Mineo. The police suspected a 'homosexual motivation' (whatever that was supposed to mean) for the murder but this predictably turned out to be a blind alley. In 1979, a pizza deliveryman named Lionel Ray Williams was sentenced to 57 years in prison for killing Mineo. Williams was a violent robber with a long list of crimes.

Williams was pretty dumb because he was in jail at the time and kept boasting to other prisoners that he had killed someone famous. The other prisoners obviously ratted him and it came to light that that Williams was probably the person who had stabbed Sal to death in 1976. I say 'probably' because Williams was black and eyewitnesses that night say they saw a white man running away from the murder scene. Williams, when charged, said he'd never heard of Sal Mineo and had no idea who he was. The upshot of all of this is that there remains a slight sense of mystery about Sal's death - despite the apparent murderer serving time for the crime.

CORY MONTEITH

The Canadian born actor and singer Corey Monteith was best known for his role as Finn Hudson on the Fox television series Glee. Monteith had appeared in many TV shows like Stargate Atlantis and Flash Gordon and his movie roles included Final Destination 3 and Deck the Halls. It was Glee though that made him a star. Despite his fame and success, Monteith had a troubled youth and battled drink and drugs problems.

Sadly, his demons got the better of him in 2013. He was found dead in his room at the Fairmont Pacific Rim hotel in Vancouver. The inquest revealed that he had died of a heroin overdose. There was also codeine and morphine in his system and two empty bottles of champagne in his hotel room. He was

31 years-old. Monteith had been trying to get clean and sober and it is speculated that, after a period of sobriety, his tolerance for drugs was low and so this binge proved fatal. It was not a suicide.

The fifth season of Glee was delayed after Corey's death but eventually went ahead. In the end they had his character Finn die in the show but did not give any cause of death.

Corey's character was frequently mentioned in the show as a tribute. Cory Monteith's last ever television appearance was as himself in a 2013 episode of Masterchef.

Sadly, Corey Monteith was not the only cast member of Glee to meet an untimely end. Seven years later his Glee co-star Naya Rivera drowned after she failed to return from a boating excursion on Lake Piru near her home in California. She was with her son at the time - who was found alone on the boat. It is believed that Naya Rivera got into trouble battling a rip current and managed to get her son on the boat but then drowned. She was 33 years-old.

After member of the Glee cast who died young was Mark Salling. Salling shot to fame through his role as Noah "Puck" Puckerman in the popular TV show. Salling's career was destroyed though when he was arrested in 2015 for possession of child pornography. In 2018, he took his own life and was found hanging near a field. It was near the end of 2015, Salling was arrested for possession of child pornography. Over 50,000 child porn images were found on his computer by the police. It is believed that a girlfriend tipped the authorities off to his crimes.

As you might imagine, the charges destroyed Salling's career and he was axed from a movie he was making at the time. Salling had his passport confiscated while he awaited sentencing and was expected to get a prison term. There was more trouble for Salling because women started coming out of the woodwork and accusing him of sexual assault. There were also rumours that he was deeply troubled (even before the child porn charges) and had attempted suicide in the past. Salling killed himself by way of hanging near a little league field before he could be sentenced. Salling clearly saw no future for himself. All he had to look forward to was prison and then life as a registered sex offender. He knew his acting career was over and his reputation was disgraced so he simply decided to end it all.

MARILYN MONROE

The actress Marilyn Monroe, probably the most famous female sex symbol of all time, died in 1962 at the age of 36 from an apparent overdose of sleeping pills. There are of course though numerous theories about her death and many believe she was murdered. It has been alleged that Monroe was under CIA surveillance due to her intimate knowledge of the Kennedy brothers and alleged links to communists (which presumably stemmed from her marriage to the left-wing writer Arthur Miller). In his book Marilyn At Rainbow's End, Darwin Porter claims that Monroe was killed by the mob. Darwin believes that Mafia boss Sam Giancana had Marilyn killed - possibly at the behest of one of the Kennedy brothers. The book claims that five Mafia enforcers used chloroform on Marilyn and then administered drugs to make it look like an overdose or suicide.

Theories on Marilyn's premature death continue to abound and probably always will. The mob story even includes an allegation that Marilyn's little black book detailing her sexual encounters with famous people was stolen during the murder to protect their identities. Jack Lemmon said it was completely true that Marilyn Monroe had an affair with JFK. "One day I was coming back home and there's this helicopter doing a low lazy circle above it. And there were these guys in funny suits and funny glasses, standing around watching Marilyn Monroe and JFK having a frolic in the pool. So whatever stories you've heard about Marilyn, that one is true: it was a big affair for her and she was in a deep relationship with JFK. Whether he thought the same, we'll never know. I think for sure she shouldn't have got mixed up in the Kennedy clan. But she was the type of girl that looked straight into trouble and no one could ever advise her."

Despite her fame it seems that Marilyn was not the most popular person in Hollywood. The director Billy Wilder found the unreliability and persistent lateness of Marilyn Monroe so annoying and unprofessional that when his famous movie Some Like It Hot finished shooting he didn't bother to invite Monroe to the wrap party. Tony Curtis added to the general sense of irritation Monroe seemed to have created on the set by saying that kissing Monroe in the film had been like kissing Hitler. Eddie Fisher once said of Marilyn - "Marilyn Monroe was a serious player. She used people — she played them off, and I was a victim, too. When I first met her at the start of the Fifties, she made a beeline for me and asked me out on many occasions for a date. But she wasn't the 'Marilyn' creation then — pretty, yes, but fake. And that was the problem."

The real truth is that we simply don't know in Marilyn was murdered or simply died an unhappy death thanks to an overdose (which may or may not have been intentional). It's a mystery that seems destined to be the subject of many more books for years to come.

ERIN MORAN

Erin Moran shot to fame at the age of thirteen as Joanie Cunningham in the sitcom Happy Days. She even appeared in the (much maligned) spin-off show Joanie Loves Chachi before returning to Happy Days for its final run of episodes in 1984. When the show ended though, Erin Moran discovered life in Hollywood for former child stars can be a very unforgiving and cold hearted experience. The phone stopped ringing and she found it almost impossible to get any acting work. She also battled drug addiction and quickly blew through all the money she had earned on Happy Days. Erin said she suffered greatly from depression when Happy Days ended and her acting career floated away into the etha.

To take a detour for a moment, I'll always remember Erin Moran for the 1981 horror film film Galaxy of Terror. Galaxy of Terror is a 1981 science fiction horror film produced by Roger Corman and directed by Bruce D Clark. This is another in the slew of Alien copycats that followed in the wake of Ridley Scott's classic. Galaxy of Terror is very low budget but it does have some things going for it. James Cameron worked on the special effects and designs and the cast is not bad at all. It includes Sid Haig and a young Robert Englund.

The premise of Galaxy of Terror has a ship sent to the desolate planet of Morganthus to investigate what happened to another ship which crashed there. The crew of the Morganthus are dragged to the surface and have a most unpleasant experience when they start to be killed off by mysterious dark forces which seem to be able to tap into their darkest fears. Erin's character meets a most brutal end in the movie and Taaffe O'Connell is raped by a gigantic maggot. This was a pretty controversial scene because Taaffe's character seems to be quite enjoying her demise. Personally, I can think of better ways to go.

Happy Days ended in 1984 and after Erin simply couldn't get any work. Happy Days co-stars like Ron Howard and Henry Winkler did fine. Tom Bosley did Father Dowling Mysteries while Scott Baio did Charles in Charge and Diagnosis Murder. Poor old Erin Moran though was seemingly forgotten by Hollywood. Winkler and Scott Baio were even in the Ron Howard show Arrested Development but Erin Moran never got to appear in it (despite speculation that she would). Most of Erin's television appearances after Happy Days were as herself rather than as an actor.

In 2011, Erin and some of her Happy Days co-stars sued CBS

for money they believed was owed to them from profits and merchandise. Erin received just $65,000 in the settlement. This money didn't last very long and she was reported to be homeless at one point. In 2017, at the age of 56, Erin Moran died after being diagnosed with squamous cell carcinoma. She had been living in a trailer park and had run out of money. Moran's life had been a sobering journey from immense fame and success to poverty and obscurity.

VIC MORROW

The fantasy anthology series The Twilight Zone is one of the most famous and iconic shows in American television history. The show ended in 1964 and its creator Rod Serling sadly died far too young in 1975. In the early 1980s, Steven Spielberg (red hot at the time thanks to Raiders of the Lost Ark and E.T.) decided to make a big screen anthology version of The Twilight Zone and hired Joe Dante and George Miller to direct segments. The other two segments would be directed by Spielberg and his friend John Landis. Thanks to films like Animal House and An American Werewolf in London, Landis was one of the hottest young directors in Hollywood. Spielberg and Landis were such good friends that Spielberg even made a cameo in The Blues Brothers for Landis.

The Twilight Zone movie was something of a vanity project for Landis and Spielberg and they couldn't wait to get started. They both loved The Twilight Zone and relished the chance to bring it to the big screen. Spielberg planned to direct a remake of The Monsters Are Due On Maple Street for the movie while Dante and Miller were also assigned classic TV episodes to update. Landis, eager to outdo the others, decided to come up with an original story called Time Out. The story was about a racist bigot who must experience persecution at the sharp end when he is sent back in time to Nazi Europe and Vietnam. Landis cast the actor Vic Morrow as the lead of his segment Time Out. Morrow, now in his fifties, was best known for the old TV show Combat! but his career was rather in the doldrums by 1982. Morrow naturally jumped at the unexpected chance to be in a big movie like The Twilight Zone and thought this could resurrect his career. Little did he know though that the movie would actually cost him his life in horrendous fashion.

The Twilight Zone film was completely overshadowed by a horrific helicopter accident on the set which killed Vic Morrow and two child extras (Renee Chen and My-ca Dinh Le) during the shooting of the John Landis contribution Time Out. Landis and his team had secretly paid the families of the child extras under the table and then used the children on a dangerous night shoot (this was all in violation of California's child labor laws). During a sequence set in war torn Vietnam, Vic Morrow was required to carry the two child extras across a wind machine lashed river as explosions went off around them and a helicopter loomed overhead. Morrow (who was no spring chicken) and the child extras should not have been doing this dangerous stunt.

As the helicopter hovered into the shot, Landis kept shouting for the helicopter to get lower. Tragedy struck when the rotor blade was hit by debris from one of the explosions and the pilot lost control. The chopper violently and suddenly flipped over into the river and landed right on top of Morrow and the child actors. The children were killed instantly and Vic Morrow was decapitated by the rotor blade. A member of the crew later found Morrow's head floating in the river. This was probably the most gruesome and upsetting accident in Hollywood history. It was made all the worse by the fact that two of the victims were innocent children.

The tragic accident swiftly ended the friendship between Twilight Zone's producer Steven Spielberg (who not present on the set that night and devastated and angry when he found out what had happened - it's a pity Spielberg wasn't on the set because there is no way he would have permitted Landis to be so reckless)) and John Landis and led to a ten year manslaughter case in the courts. To the surprise of most observers, Landis somehow managed to evade any serious charges for the accident - despite the fact that he had needlessly put his lead actor and two child extras at risk simply because of his determination to capture a great shot for his film. Two books were written about the Twilight Zone accident and they both painted John Landis as a bombastic, reckless, and dangerous egomaniac. According to the book Outrageous Conduct, Landis even used live ammunition on the set of Time Out because he wanted it to look more realistic when plants and trees were shot up during the Vietnam segment.

The power and influence of Steven Spielberg was evident in the way that he avoided any participation in the court case and investigation which followed. Spielberg's underlings were also elusive and unhelpful when it came to the accident investigation. It was left to John Landis to carry the can (and rightly so one might argue) but - all the same - it was fascinating to see how Spielberg was practically untouchable thanks to his powerful status in Hollywood. Joe Dante, who directed a segment in the movie, had to give a deposition for one of the civil cases but Spielberg - who was both a director AND producer on the film - did not. That didn't make any sense and illustrated how Spielberg was shielded from the fallout.

Bizarrely, the Twilight Zone film was not scrapped. Spielberg eventually adapted the whimsical and gentle Kick the Can so that he could complete his contribution to the film in a matter of days and then wash his hands of the whole tragic affair. The movie was eventually put out with little promotion. It is not, for understandable reasons, a picture that Spielberg or Landis ever want to discuss these days. The oddest thing about Twilight Zone: The Movie is that they left in the John Landis segment with Vic Morrow. This does make the movie a rather ghoulish experience now with the knowledge of what happened during the production.

The career of John Landis never quite recovered from the awful Twilight Zone tragedy. Despite the success he had directing Michael Jackson's famous Thriller horror music video, Landis found his status in Hollywood reduced thanks to the Twilight Zone affair and the poor reception of films like Into the Night and Spies Like Us. He never really managed to get back to the Hollywood top table again although he did have a solid box-office hit with the 1988 Eddie Murphy comedy Coming to America. By the 1990s though Landis was pretty washed up. He never fufilled his early potential. The fracture of his friendship and partnership with Spielberg diminished his status in Hollywood. When some Hollywood directors wrote a public letter of support to Landis after the accident, Spielberg was notably not among them. Brian De Palma also declined to support Landis and expressed the view that Landis had been highly irresponsible to use children in a night shoot that involved explosions and helicopters.

Vic Morrow was the father of Jennifer Jason Leigh - who later became a famous actress. Both of Morrow's daughters and the families of the child actors received undisclosed damages out of court as a result of the accident. It was scant consolation though for their losses. John Landis came off as arrogant and unsympathetic during the trial. He tried to pass the blame off to special effects people. The recklessness and arrogance of Landis had put Morrow and the children in danger in the first place and that is something that John Landis will always have to live with. The deaths of Vic Morrow and Renee Chen and My-ca Dinh Le remain among the most disturbing and tragic in Hollywood history.

Helicopters have been responsible for a large number of deaths in Hollywood. A young stuntman was burned to death in a helicopter crash on the TV show Airwolf, the director Boris Sagal died after walking into a helicopter blade shooting the TV miniseries World War III (such is Hollywood that shooting resumed with a new director the next day!), and eight people died in a helicopter crash on the set of the Chuck Norris film Braddock: Missing in Action III. This is merely the tip of the iceberg. The advent of CGI has reduced the danger posed by helicopters on film sets though. If CGI had been around in 1982, Vic Morrow and Renee Chen and My-ca Dinh Le wouldn't have been killed because John Landis could have just digitally added a helicopter and explosions into the sequence in post-production.

Sadly, terrible accidents on movie sets have happened both before and after the awful Twilight Zone tragedy. Noah's Ark is a 1928 film directed by Michael Curtiz and written by Darryl F Zanuck. This is a prime example of how appearing in a big epic film in Old Hollywood could be a dangerous line of work at the best of times. Shooting the climax of this movie involved 600,000 gallons of water and tragedy soon abounded. Five extras drowned shooting the flood sequence and there were a number of serious injuries from extras being thrown around by the water. One extra had to have a limb amputated and there were broken bones all over the place. Other thirty ambulances were required on the set and the lead actress was left with a bout of pneumonia. Noah's Ark forced Hollywood to introduce new safety standards for film productions and spare a thought for the poor extras who were risking life and limb to bring these Hollywood epics to life.

In 2014, a film called Midnight Rider was shooting in Georgia. The film required a scene where William Hurt's character has a dream that he is in bed on some railroad tracks. Despite not securing permission, the director Randall Miller decided to shoot this scene on a real rural railway bridge. William Hurt had severe misgivings about the scene but was told it would be fine. Nothing could be further from the truth. As the scene was being shot, a real train suddenly appeared and thundered towards Hurt and the crew on the tracks. They all scrambled for safety but - tragically - camera assistant Sarah Jones was struck by the train and lost her life. Randall Miller later pleaded guilty to felony involuntary manslaughter and criminal trespass and spent a year in prison. One might argue that John Landis was lucky not to receive a similar fate.

BRITTANY MURPHY

Brittany Murphy was an American actress who appeared in many big mainstream films after beginning life as a child actor in the early 1990s. She had roles in movies like Clueless, Girl Interrupted, Drop Dead Gorgeous, 8 Miles, and Sin City among others. She was also a singer and a good stage actress. Cute and quirky, Brittany Murphy was a pretty big star in her day. Murphy was also very versatile as an actress. She could do both comedy and drama and she also proved with movies like Cherry Falls that she could play the lead and carry a film. Despite her blonde good lucks, Murphy was perfectly willing to play different sorts of roles and as a consequence of this she avoided typecasting. Bright and popular, the sky seemed to be the limit for Brittany Murphy.

Behind the scenes though there was gossip about her private life. When she lost a lot of weight rumours of cocaine abuse surfaced although Murphy denied these stories. Brittany Murphy was somewhat unfathomable and kooky in real life. She ended up marrying a portly and unknown British screenwriter named Simon Monjack in 2007. Monjack's only real credit was the movie Factory Girl but the makers of this film later said that Monjack contributed nothing to the story. Murphy and Monjack were rarely seen together in public and seemed to be quite reclusive - certainly by Hollywood standards. They had a strange arrangement too because they lived in the same house as Brittany Murphy's mother Sharon.

A 2021 documentary about Brittany Murphy alleged that Simon Monjack was basically a manipulative con artist who saw Murphy as his meal ticket. He cut her off from her friends, fired her agents and managers, and took control of her money (blowing his way through $3 million of it in the process). Monjack would give Brittany's mother gifts of jewellery to keep her sweet but it all turned out to be fake. It was reported that Monjack once got Brittany Murphy fired from a movie by turning up on the set drunk. He was clearly not a tremendous help to her career. In fact, you might argue that Monjack ruined Brittany Murphy's career in the end.

On December 20, 2009, Sharon found Brittany Murphy had collapsed unconscious in the bathroom and called for an ambulance. Murphy was taken to hospital where she died of cardiac arrest. She was only 32 years-old. Pneumonia was the official cause of her death according to the coroner's report. Murphy was suffering from anaemia — a bodily condition when blood lacks the fundamental healthy red blood cells known as haemoglobin (responsible for binding with oxygen). The report found Murphy wasn't abusing drugs or alcohol at the time of her death but there were trace amounts of Vicodin and other drugs found in her body. Brittany Murphy was one of those people who literally had a drug store of medicines and pills at home. Some were prescribed and others were purchased under the counter (so to speak).

Murphy also had a history of diabetes and had complained of stomach pains a few weeks before her death. There was a bizarre and puzzling coda to this story when Brittany Murphy's husband Simon Monjack died of similar symptoms in the same house several months later. This led to theories that Murphy and Monjack had fallen ill because of toxic mold present in the property. This theory though, despite being believed by Sharon Murphy, could not be proven. There was another twist when Brittany Murphy's father Angelo Bertolotti alleged that his daughter had been poisoned and insisted that the authorities perform tests to investigate his theory. This theory though was also never verified or proven.

Brittany Murphy's mother and Monjack made a bizarre appearance on Larry King after Brittany's death and both appeared to be rather addled. It was said that they slept in the same bed. The documentary about Murphy alleged that her health was impacted by Monjack making her lose weight (which was ironic because he was overweight himself) and their addiction to uppers and downers. Brittany Murphy was said to have been increasingly spaced out and frail before her death on movie sets and at premieres. A prominent gossip columnist predicted at the start of 2009 that Brittany would be the next Hollywood celebrity to die prematurely. It was a rather ghoulish prediction perhaps but - sadly - turned out to be true.

Brittany Murphy's career was slightly in the doldrums when she died (in the last phase of her career she seemed to be making straight to DVD and television movies) but it seems certain that someone with her talent could have turned that around - especially if she'd managed to ditch Simon Monjack. Sadly, that chance was denied her by the cruel hand of fate.

HEATHER O'ROURKE

Heather O'Rourke was a child actress who got her big break when Steven Spielberg saw her having lunch with her mother in the MGM commissary and went over and offered her the part of Carol Anne Freeling in the 1982 horror film Poltergeist he was writing and producing. O'Rourke was six years old at the time and had already appeared in an episode of Fantasy Island. Poltergeist was a huge hit in 1982 and made Heather O'Rourke one of the most recognisable children in America. She was most famous for her very blonde hair - which often appeared white onscreen.

After the huge success of Poltergeist, Heather O'Rourke became a busy and in demand child actor, appearing not only in two Poltergeist sequels but also TV shows like CHiPs and Matt Houston. In 1985, Heather was in the television movie Surviving: A Family in Crisis. Surviving: A Family in Crisis had a pretty amazing cast in retrospect. It starred Molly Ringwald, River Phoenix, Ellen Burstyn, Paul Sorvino, and William Windom. Heather also won a young artist award for her guest role in the sitcom Webster.

Heather was pretty intelligent and sassy for her age. When she did an interview for Poltergeist III she said she didn't think the film was very scary. While that probably didn't endear her to studio executives it showed that she wasn't afraid to venture forth with any opinions she might have. Heather O'Rourke came from a good family and was very bright. She seemed to have as good a chance as anyone of avoiding the child star jinx and keeping her feet on the ground as she got older.

Heather O'Rourke's life was to be tragically short though. She died of septic shock on the 1st of February 1988 at the Children's Hospital in San Diego. Heather O'Rourke was only twelve when she died. Her health had been bad for some time because she contracted giardiasis (a parasitic disease) from well water near her home and also had Crohn's disease. What was presumed to be a bout of ordinary flu launched Heather O'Rourke into cardiac arrest during the drive to the local hospital as bacterial toxins set loose by a bowel obstruction made their way into her bloodstream. She passed away on the operating table.

The official cause of death was cardiac-pulmonary arrest and septic shock, the result of an undetected intestinal blockage. Heather's mother launched a wrongful death lawsuit and claimed that medical negligence had contributed to her daughter's death. It was a dreadfully tragic case. Heather had just finished shooting Poltergeist III and had recently been to Disneyland to celebrate. Her sudden death was a terrible shock for her family and those that had worked with her.

Heather died while Poltergeist III was in post-production. Some reshoots were required to change the ending and so an eleven year-old child actor named Heather Holty had to stand in as Heather's character Carol Anne Freeling. The director Gary Sherman didn't want to finish the film after Heather's death but studio pressure apparently forced him to complete it. Poltergeist III received poor reviews and was a box-office flop. Heather's comments on the set that she didn't think the movie was very scary turned out to be right.

The premature deaths of Heather O'Rourke and fellow Poltergeist cast member Dominique Dunne have led to theories of a 'Poltergeist Curse' but these deaths seem more like random and awful tragedies than anything. JoBeth Williams, Craig T. Nelson, and Oliver Robins, who played the other members of the Freeling family in Poltergeist, are all still very much alive and would appear to rebuff any claims about a supernatural jinx.

Other evidence for the alleged curse involves Julian Beck, who starred as Kane in Poltergeist II: The Other Side, dying of stomach cancer months before the film even came out in theatres and Will Sampson, the actor who performed the exorcism, dying of malnutrition and postoperative kidney failure at age 53. In 2009, Lou Perryman, who played Pugsley in the original film was murdered in his own home by an ex-convict with an axe.

RIVER PHOENIX

River Phoenix met his end in 1993 outside of the Viper Room - a Los Angeles nightclub owned by Johnny Depp. Phoenix was one of the most famous young stars in Hollywood and destined for a long and lucrative career. He was often compared to James Dean and famous for films like Stand By Me and Indiana Jones and the Last Crusade (in which Phoenix played the young Indy in the opening scenes). Phoenix was only 23 when he died of a drugs overdose outside of the Viper Room. River Phoenix was always regarded to be one of the most clean cut stars in Hollywood. He was a vegan environmentalist who was said to avoid alcohol. His family were famous for avoiding the Hollywood limelight. If anyone was likely to avoid the pitfalls of Hollywood it was surely River Phoenix.

All was not quite what it seemed though with River Phoenix. His parents were hippies who were once part of a religious cult. The family never had any money but that all changed when River became a child actor and started doing commercials. It is said that as he grew-up River began to feel great pressure in his position as the family cash cow. There were a lot of stories about him having an eating disorder and gorging himself on chocolate binges. Sadly, River developed a taste for things much more dangerous than cho66colate in the end. Despite his clean cut image as a bohemian Hollywood outsider River was actually the tragic cliche of a young Hollywood star.

He and his friends were frequent users of hard drugs and loved trawling seedy nightclubs. He died after injecting a 'speedball' of heroin and cocaine. His last words were - "I don't feel so good. I think I'm OD'ing." There are whispers that his drink was spiked with GBH (gamma hydroxybutyrate - a metabolite that functions as a depressant to the central nervous system, which means it functions as a relaxant). River's brother Joaquin Phoenix, who became a famous actor himself, was present the night River died and made the call to the emergency services when his brother collapsed.

The tragic night in question, River had met his girlfriend (and actress) Samantha Mathis for a drink. Though it hadn't been their original plan, they ended up going to the Viper Room club. Mathis said that one point River seemed to get into a fight with another man in the club and they were both thrown out by a doorman. River then started going into convulsions outside. Mathis went back inside to get help while Joaquin called 911. It was too late though and paramedics couldn't do anything. Mathis said that although she never saw River take drugs that night she was scared at how high he seemed to be in the end. At the time of his death River had eleven days of shooting left on a movie called Dark Blood. It sat on the shelf for many years after he passed away unexpectedly.

Martha Plimpton, an actress who was the former girlfriend of River Phoenix, was very angry at his death and felt a lot of people shared the blame. "I don't want to be comforted by his death. I think it's right that I'm angry about it, angry at the people who helped him stay sick, and angry at River. We had five million talks about his compulsive personality. You would have thought he was 90 and had died in his sleep. The people who were saying this felt tremendous guilt that they had contributed to his death."

River's last two films (Silent Tongue, Dark Blood) were released after his death. At the time of his death he was about to start shooting the film Interview with the Vampire for the director Neil Jordan. River was due to play Daniel Molloy (the interviewer who frames the film) but was replaced by Christian Slater after he died. Slater, in what was a classy move, donated his salary for Interview with the Vampire to two of River's favourite charities. Trivia - the original Phoenix family surname was 'Bottom' but they changed it to Phoenix in the seventies. River Bottom doesn't have quite the same ring does it?

SYLVIA PLATH

The American poet and writer Sylvia Plath took her own life in London on February 11, 1963. She was thirty years-old and depressed after the collapse of her marriage to the British poet Ted Hughes. Plath stuck her head in the oven and turned the gas on. She had opened the windows to the rooms where her young children were sleeping to ensure they would survive. Plath was one of those people who was more famous in death than life - which she probably would have found annoying. Her poems are highly regarded today and she wrote a pretty good novel called The Bell Jar.

Plath kept a journal her whole adult life ('my lusts and my little ideas... my Sargasso') and scribbled furiously on anything to hand to create a repository of her imagination. Because there is no definitive biography of Plath (though many have vainly tried) or indeed autobiography The Unabridged Journals of Sylvia Plath retains a singular importance in any study of the writer or attempt to understand who she was. It is though an autobiography in a mythological sense and despite her day to day streams of consciousness Plath somehow manages to remain enigmatic and hazily ephemeral. The journals were originally published in 1982 (nearly 20 years after she committed suicide in London) but were heavily edited by her estranged husband Ted Hughes.

About 50% of the updated version - which draws heavily on her college journals and previously sealed documents - is new material and Plath emerges from the book as a taller and more vivid figure. Plath was exceptionally neurotic and used her journal as a litany of dreams, directives and imperatives - confessing her deepest fears and greatest hopes. She throws around a lot of ideas for stories and poems in the journals and those are generally interesting because Plath is experimenting and trying desperately to find her own voice. It was only near the end of her short life that she truly succeeded in doing so.

Although we tend to think of Sylvia Plath as quite a gloomy and serious figure (often, but not always, looking sullen and sulky in photographs) she is often self-deprecating about her life and writing efforts in the journals. Plath's love of language and descriptive passages make the book very descriptive and dreamy to read at times as you wallow in her frequently fantastical and often atmospheric flourishes. Plath was deeply affected by her father dying when she was only eight years old and had suicidal impulses from a young age, ending up in a battery of special hospitals. She plunged all of her despair and problems into her poetry and journals - the explanation for why her work was so dark and striking.

The journals start in 1950 and end several months before Plath's suicide. Plath had a sharp tongue and even people who remained close to her right to the end sometimes received a pasting in her journal. These occasional but vituperous lashes are more prevalent here than in the previous Hughes edited version. It's not always pretty but it is compelling. Amusingly, you also learn in the unabridged volume that in the 1950s

Plath submitted material from herself and Hughes for food company jingles, such was their threadbare financial plight at the time. That nugget of information was obviously something that Ted Hughes was rather eager to brush under the carpet in 1982 as it does not appear in the earlier version of this.

You get more of a tangible sense here of Plath in this enjoyably expansive version of her journals - both good and bad. She could be funny, moving, eccentric, irritating, self-indulgent, likeable, difficult, cruel, kind, complex, and so on. Despite all the navel gazing and internal monologues, you do pick up details about Plath's more mundane day to day life though that are always interesting. She would drink two cups of strong coffee in the morning and get back into bed to with her 'coffee vision' to think and ponder. She loved beaches and walks in the countryside and her two favourite things to do to break up the monotony of writing were taking naps and pottering about in the kitchen. Plath's last days were spent in London where she had always wanted to live because she loved the parks. She disliked American suburbs and found the American countryside too remote and alienating.

The book affords us the opportunity to gain a portrait of Plath in all of her various incarnations; adolescent, student, young woman, poet, wife, mother. This aspect to the journals is much greater here than in the earlier version. Ted Hughes is generally cast as the villain in most telling of the Sylvia Plath story, his infidelities often cited as a crucial factor in her eventual despair and unhappiness. There have been books that have been somewhat more sympathetic to Hughes (painting Plath as something of a wolf herself with no grasp on reality) but they are in the minority. Despite the intense enduring interest in Plath and her life, Hughes always remained completely silent about her (until Birthday Letters) and frequently received much scorn from Plath admirers for having an affair when they were married and destroying the last part of her journals after her death, an act Hughes says he did to spare their children

In 1998, the Ted Hughes poem collection Birthday Letters was published. The poems are all about his relationship with Sylvia Plath. Given the long silence by Hughes on Plath, Birthday Letters (which contains 88 poems) was therefore a very big deal when it was published and eagerly anticipated. 'You are ten years dead,' says Hughes in one of the first poems (Visit). 'It is only a story. Your story. My story.'

What is obvious reading Birthday Letters is that Hughes held deep affection for Plath and was somewhat tormented by her memory to the end of his life (he was dying when Birthday Letters was published). There are many poignant moments in the poems where Hughes is suddenly reminded of Plath by something random and memories come rushing back of a particular room or place where they were together. One of the early poems has an incredibly sad bit where Hughes is working at his desk and one of his children comes in and asks him where her mother is. One of the things I liked about Birthday Letters was the way that the poems seem to be arranged chronologically in terms of their relationship (rather than the actual date of the poems) like a story, beginning with their first meetings and then charting Plath's life with Hughes and beyond.

Hughes recalls seeing a picture of Fulbright Scholars at Charing Cross Station when he was 22 and wondering now if Plath, with her 'Veronica Lake bangs', was amongst them, and remembers an early evening out they had together, walking past bomb craters from the war on the way home. The poems build a portrait of their life together with many details of Plath's likes and dislikes and habits. Hughes remembers her love of drawing, using an Ouija Board together, and how her reactions to birds, nature and wildlife in England made it feel like he was seeing some of these things for the first time too. 'Through your eyes it was foreign. Plain hedge hawthorns were peculiar aliens. You were a camera. Recording reflections you could not fathom.' You do get the sense that these were two almost mythic figures who were always slightly in awe of one another.

One of the longest poems is called The 59th Bear and is an incredible memory piece by Hughes where he recalls some of the images they saw traveling through America together. 'We counted bears - as if all we wanted were more bears. Yellowstone. Folded us into its robe, its tepees. Of mountain and conifer. To me as to you. Paradise, we saw.' There is an interesting poem called The Table that begins with Hughes remembering the time when he made a writing desk for Plath. 'You bent over it, euphoric. With your Nescafe every morning. Like an animal, smelling the wild air.' The poem ends with Hughes taking a swipe at the 'peanut-crunchers' (a reference to Plath's poem Lady Lazarus) who '...can stare. At the ink-stains, the sigils. Where you engraved your letters to him.' It's essentially Hughes saying that people who think they know Sylvia Plath and what happened between him and her are mistaken and mere onlookers.

I found the early poems the most moving perhaps, the fascinating descriptions of Plath ('Your eyes. Squeezed in your face, a crush of diamonds. Incredibly bright, bright as a crush of tears') as she first appeared to him when they met, and the glimpses of their life together. You form pictures as the poems continue on to touch upon things like holidays in America, moving to Devon and living in an old isolated farmhouse, and Plath's sulky mood one day because she misses the beach she remembers from growing up and feels a great urge to be there again.

Birthday Letters becomes much darker towards the end and Hughes incorporates some of the imagery from Plath's poems and again seems to have a swipe at those who continue to gawp at the details of Plath's life and death. As someone with Plath journals and biographies sitting on my bookshelf I suppose I must be one of those gawpers or 'peanut-crunchers' myself. Dreamers is a fascinating poem too as it is apparently about a meeting between Plath and the woman Hughes left her for. 'She fascinated you. Her eyes caressed you. Melted a weeping glitter at you. Her German the dark undercurrent. In her Kensington jewelers' elocution.'

The thing that comes through strongest from the poems is that Hughes thought about Plath constantly for the rest of his life and many of the poems are powerful because of this. The most affecting thing about Birthday Letters is the sense that Hughes was setting down little details that perhaps only he could remember so they would be saved beyond his life. Memories like the way Plath's hair used to fall over her face sometimes, her hands and expression when she played old songs on the piano and just something as simple as her sitting in the back of a class clutching a big mug of coffee. It's this Sylvia Plath that you imagine invaded Hughes' thoughts when he was alone at his desk years after her death or his dreams when he went to bed at night. Birthday Letters is a must buy for any fans of Ted Hughes or anyone interested in Sylvia Plath. I found the book fascinating and often quite moving.

DANA PLATO

Dana Plato shot to fame at the age of 13 when she won a part in the hugely popular seventies and eighties sitcom Diff'rent Strokes. Plato had to choose between an ice-skating career and acting and, all things considered, she probably should have stuck with the ice-skating. Plato played Kimberley in Diff'rent Strokes. Prior to this she had small parts in Exorcist II: The Heretic, Return to Boggy Creek, California Suite, and The Six Million Dollar Man. Believe it or not though it was Plato's appearance on The Gong Show (which was a crazy talent competition) which apparently attracted the attention of the producers of Diff'rent Strokes.

Dana Plato, who had wholesome girl next door looks (Plato looks a bit like a young Chelsea Clinton in some of her photographs), looked set for a long career in Hollywood but this didn't turn out to be the case at all. Plato was booted off of Diff'rent Strokes for getting pregnant (her character Kimberley was supposed to be younger than Plato and the producers simply didn't want a teen pregnancy storyline in the show -

which was odd because they usually loved shoehorning social issues into Diff'rent Strokes!) and her career went nowhere fast - thanks in large part to her drug problems.

Plato returned to Diff'rent Strokes for some guest appearances but after it ended in 1986 Dana found that her telephone rarely seemed to ring anymore. Her acting CV became a barren desert with the occasional wind blown tumbleweed. In the tradition of numerous other washed-up former child stars she was reduced to doing cheapie straight to video type movies that hardly anyone watched. Dana was rather like Erin Moran in this respect. It must be pretty rough to come out of a big TV show and then find that literally no one wants to hire you anymore.

After a supporting role in a forgotten 1989 film with the highly original title Prime Suspect (an interesting cast for this one - it featured Doug McClure, Frank Stallone, and Michael Parks!) 1992 saw Dana lend her voice to the video game Night Trap and star in something called Bikini Beach Race with the now disgraced porn actor Ron Jeremy. Other long forgotten Plato trash classics included Lethal Cowboy and martial arts obscurity Blood Boxer. In 1995, Plato tried to cash in on her long lost sitcom fame by starring in the soft core lesbian drama Different Strokes: The Story of Jack and Jill...and Jill. Literally no one saw any of these movies Dana was making. She was trapped in the Phantom Zone of Hollywood invisibility.

Dana lost custody of her son and even had breast augmentation in the hope of becoming a Playboy model. The nadir for Plato came in 1992 when she was arrested for trying to rob a video store with a plastic gun. It was a pretty bizarre story and for this reason made the headlines in the United States. This was literally the first time Dana had experienced any fame since Diff'rent Strokes ended but - alas - it was for all the wrong reasons. This eccentric robbery only netted Plato a paltry $160. She was clearly a woman who needed help. Dana was sentenced to five years probation for the robbery but weeks later got into more trouble when she was arrested for forging a valium prescription. This landed her in jail for thirty days.

Sadly, you probably didn't need to be Nostradamus to predict that Dana Plato wouldn't make old bones. She was found dead in her RV home in 1999. The verdict was an overdose of painkillers and other medication. She was just 34 years old. The money and fame she once enjoyed was merely a distant memory by the time of her sad death. Dana's former mother-in-law was reported to claim that Dana had been murdered. Her finger of suspicion was aimed at Dana's fiancée Robert Menchaca.

A sleazeball promoter named Shane Bugbee had tried to cash in on Dana's death by putting a CD and booklet about her up for sale which was tastelessly titled Dana's Last Breath. It was said to include a photo of her dead body - which only Menchaca could have taken because he was there when she died. Whatever the truth it was all rather morbid and distasteful. There was a very tragic coda to this story because Dana's son Tyler committed suicide eleven years after her death at the age of 25.

When Gary Coleman paid his tribute to Dana he said that she was a wonderful woman but it was a blessing in disguise she had died because this meant there was now no chance of a Diff'rent Strokes reunion. Stay classy Gary! The chances of a Diff'rent Strokes reunion were reduced to zero when Coleman died himself. This left Todd Bridges as literally the only cast member of Diff'rent Strokes still alive. He played Willis Jackson in the show and was a successful child actor even before this big break.

Bridges found life after Diff'rent Strokes difficult and has been arrested for numerous drugs convictions. In 1989 he was charged with the murder of a Los Angeles drug dealer but was found not guilty of the charges after it was proven that he was somewhere else at the time. Despite his troubles, Bridges has managed to keep working (mostly TV movies) and these days lectures youngsters about the perils of drugs.

ELVIS PRESLEY

Elvis Presley was probably the most famous person in the world at the time of his death. Only the likes of Muhammad Ali could rival his fame. Presley's career ebbed and flowed but his fame and stature was constant. He was the King. Presley wasn't helped much though by his manager "Colonel" Tom Parker - or Andreas Cornelis van Kuijk to give his real name. Parker was a Dutchman who created a new identity for himself in the United States. It was Parker who signed Elvis up to those (mostly) terrible musical films which Elvis didn't enjoy making very much.

Sadly, Elvis never went on a world tour because Parker didn't want to leave America for fear of his secret identity being exposed. Elvis was sort of in limbo making those cheapie bland musical films. His career seemed to be stuck in third gear. What didn't help either was the new wave of British music in the form of The Beatles and Rolling Stones. These groups threatened to make Elvis look like some old rockabilly fossil of a bygone era. Parker's mistake was signing Elvis to a long term film contract churning out cheap musicals. What he should have done was get Elvis in a few big movies on a profit share deal.

As his film career petered out, Elvis threatened to become an irrelevance but the Elvis Presley '68 Comeback Special made for NBC television saw him in fine fettle and proved there was plenty of life left in Elvis. The '68 Comeback Special is the most iconic of the Elvis shows captured on film and the one where he famously wears the black leathers and looks more preposterously handsome than he'd ever been before or would be again. The image is ingrained in popular culture and remains influential (to this day, now and again, you'll get some talentless berk like Robbie Williams wear the exact same outfit and try and be Elvis in a pop video). At the time of the special, Elvis hadn't performed live for several years, something which sounds like a truly bizarre state of affairs for the most famous entertainer of the 20th Century.

When the profits on the films began to decline (even fans were losing interest in these pictures) and Elvis' music suffered as a consequence of this pivot to the silver screen, it was now apparent that a once golden career was teetering on the brink of irrelevance and something needed to be done. With Elvis apparently on the way out of the film business, NBC approached Parker about doing an Elvis special for television. Steve Binder, the eventual director of the proposed special, felt that Elvis was a unique star and performer who simply hadn't been punching his weight for a while. Why not do something to remind everyone of how great he could be?

The special was a ratings smash and made Elvis hip again before he began the Las Vegas slide into kitsch and self-parody. I love the karate kicking tassled jumpsuit Elvis from the seventies as much as anyone but we do unavoidably watch that Elvis in a slightly ironic way for comedy purposes. We know that he's drug addled and bloated, that his shows are becoming ridiculous. In the '68 Comeback Special (which by the way was just called "Elvis" when it first aired, the "Comeback" part added later), Elvis is lean and hungry. He looks great and has something to prove. This aura of physical well being and focus would fade away soon enough but it does make the '68 Comeback Special a triumph and something of a milestone in his career.

The '68 Comeback Special is essentially composed of three acts and includes over thirty (sometimes recurring obviously) performances of songs by Elvis, with a nice mixture of the familiar and not so familiar. There are songs presented on a mock stage with background dancers and silhouette sets. All very art deco and sixties. These are big production numbers that probably look a bit dated and cheesy to modern eyes but they always sort of work with Elvis front and centre and his

Trouble/Guitar Man intro shows straight away that he has the old fire back and means business. The songs have a real sense of energy and style presented in this way and do come across as early forerunners of pop videos.

It's quite good fun to see the Elvis outfits in this section and he must surely have been the only man in the world who could carry off a red neckscarf. His music career had suffered badly during his stint in Hollywood and it is generally accepted that this '68 Comeback Special was the catalyst for Elvis dedicating himself much more to the recording side of his career and also giving him the confidence to get back on stage again for live audiences. It seems strange watching this to think that he was nervous about performing live again after so long and actually had to be talked into doing this show ("Colonel" Parker also did his best to wreck the whole enterprise by suggesting to NBC that Elvis should do a Christmas special for them instead and just sing Christmas Carols for a couple of hours in a Santa suit).

This fantastic comeback though was somewhat squandered by Parker then signing Elvis up to endless Las Vegas casino shows. So began the final era of Elvis. This was the camp era with the white jumpsuits. It was fun but the physical decline of Elvis soon became apparent. He was clearly struggling with his weight and also taking enough prescription drugs to knock out an elephant. With his exhausting stage assignments something had to give in the end.

Elvis plainly wasn't taking care of himself and the people supposed to be looking after him weren't either. His biggest problem was food. It is said that because Elvis came from a very poor family (where food was never plentiful) that he overcompensated for this later in life by eating too much. What didn't help either was that his diet was atrocious. He was famously fond of fried peanut butter and banana sandwiches cooked in butter and ate way too many cheeseburgers. A favourite of Elvis was the Fool's Gold Loaf. This sandwich made from a whole loaf of French stick style Italian bread and containing a jar of peanut butter, a jar of grape jelly and a pound of bacon. Elvis once flew to Denver in his private jet just to order twenty of these sandwiches.

Elvis was so obsessed with food he had a closed-circuit television system trained on his kitchen. Foods that Elvis always had stocked at Graceland included Banana pudding, hot dog sausages, Pepsi, Brownies, ice cream, fudge cookies, all sorts of meat, and cream. This is not exactly what you would describe as health food. His personal cook said that Elvis usually had biscuits, bacon, eggs, and sausage for breakfast all cooked in butter. His daily calorie intake was out of control and all that meat, fried food, and sugar was dreadful for his health. Elvis weighed 255 pounds when he died. There are heavyweight boxers who weigh less than that. He was huge.

The last thing Elvis ever ate was peach ice cream with cookies. Overweight and addicted to prescription drugs, Elvis died in 1977 at the age of 42. Legend has it that he died on the toilet - which is sort of true. He was found next to the toilet. Elvis had so much food blocked in his system that using the toilet had become a horrendous ordeal. He was constipated beyond belief. The official cause of death was cited as a heart attack - likely brought on by his addiction to prescription barbiturates. All that food had hardly helped either though.

GEORGE REEVES

George Reeves played Superman in the first live action film based on the comic book character and also when the character moved to television for the popular Adventures of Superman in the 1950s. In those days you didn't have to be Henry Cavill or Chris Evans to play a superhero. Reeves wore a corset to keep his stomach in and had an awful woollen costume that irritated his skin. He had to suffer for his art to play the Man of Steel. Reeves once knocked himself out smashing through a door that he wrongly presumed was a prop. Reeves was also forced to make personal appearances as Superman and he loathed this. Because the children really did think Reeves was Superman, the actor was subject to all manner of dangers and indignities. A boy once stabbed him with a compass and another pulled a gun on him and said he wanted to know if the bullets would bounce off Superman's chest. Reeves had to persuade the boy to put the gun down by saying it would be dangerous if the bullets bounced off his chest into the crowd.

Reeves was found dead in his bedroom at the age of 45 from a gunshot wound while the Superman show was still in production in 1959. Reeves is probably the start of the "Superman curse" tag that is sometimes thrown around. There doesn't seem to be that much evidence for the curse.

I suppose the main two pieces of evidence are Christopher Reeve and Margot Kidder. Reeve was paralyzed from the neck down after being thrown from his horse in a cross-country equestrian riding event in 1995 while Kidder had well publicised battles with depression and took her own life in the end. For what it's worth, Kidder commented on the Superman 'curse' theory when she was alive and said she thought it was nonsense.

The verdict on the death of George Reeves was suicide (the motive was alleged to be the fact that Reeves was frustrated by the way his acting career had turned out) but many suspect he was murdered. Reeves was said to be having an affair with the wife of infamous Hollywood fixer Eddie Mannix. The unavoidable speculation is that Mannix had Reeves killed. Mannix worked at Metro-Goldwyn-Mayer from 1924 to 1962 and became notorious as a 'fixer'. Mannx was like the Winston Wolf of MGM. He was there to clean up the mess.

Mannix is alleged to have arranged abortions and kept Judy Garland addicted to pills. Believe it or not, it was fairly common for studios in Old Hollywood to arrange for abortions if any of their contracted actresses got pregnant - especially if the pregnancy happened out of wedlock or through an affair. Bette Davis, Joan Crawford, Judy Garland, Tallulah Bankhead, Jeanette McDonald, Lana Turner, and Dorothy Dandridge all had abortions arranged by the studios. The reason for the abortions was that the studios at the time inserted a 'morality clause' into the contracts of their stars. If an actress was involved in a scandalous (by the standards of the era) pregnancy, then this meant they had violated that morality clause. Some of these abortions had the consent of the actress (some actresses did not want a baby to stifle their career) and some were insisted upon.

As for Judy Garland, when she was still a teenager, the studio decided she was too fat and so took extraordinary measures to control her weight. She was put on a diet of coffee and soup and smoked eighty cigarettes a day to curb hunger pangs. Garland was given all manner of medication - including 'uppers' and 'downers' so that she could alternately stay up for hours or go to sleep in an instant. Garland became hooked on the prescription drugs and it affected her for the rest of her life. Mickey Rooney said that when he worked with Judy Garland they were often given pills by the studios that enabled them to work long hours without getting tired.

Mannix even resorted to blackmail on occasion to keep stars in line and was always on the scene before the police when it came to Hollywood deaths. Mannix was the general manager at MGM and enjoyed almost unlimited influence at the studio.

It was Mannix who made sure gossip columnists didn't know a star was in rehab. He covered up fights and car crashes, and fed false stories to the magazines to throw them off the trail of scandals. Mannix is even alleged to have had a hand in the death of Thelma Todd and the character assassination of Patricia Douglas after she claimed she was raped at a studio function. Mannix died in 1963.

LUCILLE RICKSEN

Lucille Ricksen was a silent era actress who was born in 1910 in Chicago. She became a child model at the age of four and was on the stage by the age of five. Her full name was Ingeborg Myrtle Elisabeth Ericksen and she was the child of Swedish immigrants. The Hollywood studio bosses clearly didn't think that Ingeborg was much of a name for a rising star so they changed it to Lucille. You could describe her as a child star (Lucille Ricksen was only fourteen when she died in 1925) but the strange thing about Ricksen is that she sometimes played adult roles. When she was put in adult clothes and make-up she resembled an adult more than a child onscreen so studios decided to use her this way. This is obviously something that seems wrong and distasteful today. It is also deeply troubling that Ricksen had to pose for risque photo shoots to promote herself and her films.

The studio pretended that Lucille was sixteen to mitigate any bad publicity about their use of her. Alarmingly, it is said that Lucille had an affair with Charlie Chaplin's thirty-eight year-old brother Syd and even had an abortion. Both the Chaplin brothers would be in prison and registered sex offenders if they were around today. They both liked young girls. There were definitely some weird things about the early eras of Hollywood. Shirley Temple began her career in Baby Burlesks. These were pre-code films made in the years before Hollywood had established a moral censorship code for productions to abide by.

Baby Burlesks were essentially film pastiches in which the cast are all children but dressed up as adults (sort of like Bugsy Malone). These short films are troubling today and quite bizarre. In one of the shorts Shirley Temple plainly appears to be playing a prostitute and the African-American kids were sometimes dressed up as natives from the jungle. In her memoir, Temple said that when kids misbehaved on the set of early films she worked on, they were made to go and sit on a block of ice as punishment.

Lucille Ricksen is a very early example of a bankable child star who was exploited by both her family and the studio purely for financial gain. Lucille was definitely the family cash cow. She was the only one bringing in any money so they all relied on her. This meant she had to constantly work and wasn't allowed to have a normal childhood. Her friends were all adults from the film industry so it was a very strange sort of childhood. Lucille was deprived the chance to just be a normal kid. She was exhausted in the end and appears increasingly fragile and ill in her movies. In just five years from 1920 to 1925 she made made around thirty-five movies and short films. That was a punishing ordeal for one so young.

The studio had taken to putting lipstick on Lucille and making her eyes darker so she could play adult roles. The strange thing about this is that her family didn't seem to object. I suppose they just wanted the money. In the 1924 film Rendezvous, thirteen year-old Lucille played the love interest of Conrad Nagel - who was forty years-old. They even have kissing scenes in the film. The makers of this film would be arrested today. Lucille was made to sign numerous contracts so the chance of a break from acting was impossible. She always had commitments to fufil. When you factor in the fact that Lucille had to travel a lot to promote the films and make personal appearances you can see how punishing this must have been in the end for a girl who was barely a teenager.

Lucille Ricksen died in 1925 of Tuberculosis and was suffering from malnutrition at the time. Ricksen really needed a long rest, medical care, and a more normal childhood but, sadly, she was chewed up and spat out by the Hollywood machine and greedy parents. She was bedridden near the end and slipped into a coma.

In 1924 she made ten films in seven months. Lucille Ricksen was ill and exhausted and her body simply couldn't take any more.

GEORGE ROSE

George Rose was a distinguished British actor with appearances in films like The Pickwick Papers, Track the Man Down, A Night to Remember, and Hawaii. He was also greatly acclaimed for his stage work and had won more awards than you've had hot dinners. In 1984, he purchased a holiday home in Sosúa, Dominican Republic and adopted a local 16 year-old teenage boy named Jaun. Rose, who was gay, had no family of his own and wanted an heir so he would have someone to leave his money to. He planned to teach Jaun about music and theatre. The kid though wasn't much of a student and didn't make any progress. In the end, George Rose decided to change his will so the kid didn't get anything. Sadly, he never got a chance to do this.

Rose had many famous friends in the acting world and was never short of work. He loved his home in Sosúa so much that he had a special clause put in his contract when he was touring a play that enabled him to take breaks so he could go back to his paradise home. His acting friends ever quite saw the appeal of his exotic hideaway. While it was a beautiful place they also found it a lonely and threatening sort of place too. There was always a whiff of violence and danger in the air. Some have suggested though that George Rose might have liked this. It is said that he used to happily live in a rough and dangerous part of New York that most actors would avoid like the plague.

On the 5th of May, 1988, George Rose was found dead in an overturned car in the Dominican Republic. Cocaine was found in his wallet and the local papers said he had a heart attack at the wheel - probably as a result of the cocaine. When they heard about the circumstances of his death, Rose's shocked friends immediately smelled a rat. They knew that Rose rarely drove and hated drugs. It all sounded bogus to them. Rose's neighbour in Sosúa, an American woman named Bea Garcia, said she went down to investigate when she heard about the accident and saw that Rose had suspicious injuries and seemed to have his arms frozen in a manner which suggested he was fending off blows. Garcia saw too that the ground where the accident took place made it unlikely the car could have overturned.

Garcia could see straight away that Rose had been murdered and that it had been made to look like an accident. She was furious when a police officer and doctor on the scene seemed complicit in the cover-up and refused to accept her claim that this was obviously a case of murder. Juan claimed that the adoption was a front for a homosexual relationship. The reality is that Rose was tortured and murdered by the boy and the boy's family. Rose had received heavy blows to the head. He was 68 years old.

Unbelievably, although the assailants were arrested they were soon released and there was no trial. The local authorities were totally corrupt and couldn't have cared less about the murder. The local press made it seem like Rose was some sexual deviant who'd got what he deserved. It was only the bravery of Bea Garcia that kicked up any fuss about this case at all and landed the murderers in prison (though sadly not for long). When the Dominican authorities tried to bully Garcia and shut her up she got the American Embassy involved and they protected her and made sure the case was heard. Sadly though justice was definitely not done in the end.

One tragic thing about about this case is that, despite his great career, the death of George Rose was barely reported in America or Europe. Some of his friends didn't even know he'd been killed in the Dominican Republic. Some of them presumed he passed away in New York or didn't even know he had died at all. Rose obviously wasn't deemed famous enough to get much ink - which is a shame and completely unfair. He was more talented that the vast majority of actors and celebrities who pass away. Jaun, the boy at the heart of this case, apparently took a trip to America with his inheritance money when he got out of prison. It's a shame he didn't get mugged while he was there.

Because of the climate in the Dominican Republic, bodies are buried quickly on the island and George Rose was dumped in an unmarked grave on what looked like a rubbish tip. It was a sad and tragic end to his life and disgraceful conduct by the local authorities.

PABLO SANTOS

Pablo Santos was a young Mexican actor best known for the short-lived sitcom Greetings from Tucson - which ran from 2002 to 2003. Greetings from Tucson wasn't destined to last for very long but it did earn praise for its mostly Latino cast - which was something of a novelty in a sitcom at the time. Santos played fifteen year-old David Tiant in the show and was the focal point of the sitcom. He earned good reviews for his comic performance in Greetings from Tucson. After the show ended, Santos appeared in big TV shows like The Shield and Alias and was in a couple of movies. He seemed to have a fairly bright future in Hollywood ahead of him. Sadly though fate was to intervene in cruel fashion.

On Friday, September 15, 2006, the now nineteen year-old Pablo Santos was with some friends on a private plane en route to General Juan N. Alvarez International Airport in Acapulco. The group were planning to celebrate Mexican independence day. After about three hours in the air a problem developed on the plane and smoke was reported in the cabin. The pilot declared that the situation was serious and decided to land the plane at Toluca International Airport in central Mexico.

On the approach to the runway the engine stopped and the plane began to go out of control. The aircraft struck a fence as it came down and then smashed through the construction site created by a building that was being demolished at the airport.

The crisis was not helped by the fact that the plane was designed to carry six people but there were seven on board. All seven occupants survived the crash landing but two were badly injured and they included Pablo Santos. He suffered bad head injuries because he had been on the floor at the time of the emergency landing and wasn't strapped in. Pablo was taken to the Issemym Medical Center but died two hours later. It was a tragic end for this promising young actor. One of his friends in the plane was put on life support and died the next day.

Aviation officials found that the plane hardly had any fuel in the tanks when it crashed and so the main theory for the tragedy was that the aircraft simply ran out of fuel. one of the survivors said that the plane's motor coughed and then then cut out and after that everything happened really fast. He said he came to to find everyone covered in blood. Santos and his friends and apparently persuaded the pilot to take an extra passenger - despite it only being designed for six. Though this didn't cause the accident it obviously wasn't a great help when the plane got into trouble. Pablo Santos was regarded in the entertainment industry to be a friendly and down to earth kid so his premature death was especially sad.

PRINCESS DIANA

Princess Diana of Wales died from a 1997 car crash in a Paris tunnel at the age of 36 and almost at once people wondered if there might have been foul play at foot. When very famous people die it is as if some people simply cannot accept this happened and look for alternatives (example - when Elvis and Michael Jackson died, some fans preferred to believe they somehow faked their own deaths). The conspiracy theories relating to the death of Diana tend to revolve around an alleged Royal Family/British Secret Service collusion that wanted the "rogue" Princess silenced lest she should cause the institution of which she belonged any more embarrassment in the future.

Mohammed Al-Fayed, the father of her lover Dodi (who also died in the tragic crash), has long claimed that foul play was behind her death and believes it was because Dodi was a Muslim. He further claims that Diana was pregnant at the time of her death and the authorities (by this I suppose he means the royal family) didn't want the child to be born. Those who believe such theories point out that it seemed to take a long time to get Diana to hospital and that her security was surprisingly light for such a global celebrity.

The car Diana was in slammed into a concrete wall at 65 mph. She survived the crash but went into cardiac arrest and, following external cardiopulmonary resuscitation, her heart started beating again. Diana's heart had been displaced to the right side of the chest, which tore the pulmonary vein and the pericardium. She was pronounced dead in hospital after extensive attempts by French doctors to save her life. An inquest later found that Diana would have died of her injuries even if she had been rushed to hospital sooner. It was a horrendous crash. The car was basically squashed like an accordion.

At the time of her death, Diana was rather estranged from the royal family and separated from Charles. She was though still popular with the British public for a variety of reasons. First of all she was very glamorous and attractive (and still only in her mid-thirties). Diana definitely had star quality - which you certainly couldn't say of Charles' preferred squeeze the dowdy Camilla Parker-Bowles. The public tended to side with Diana because was seen as a victim. It appeared in hindsight that Charles never really cared that much about her and she was basically just brought into the family to have a nice royal wedding and produce some children.

It should be noted though that Diana wasn't exactly Mother Theresa. She seemed to spend much of her time lounging around on yachts. It wasn't as if she was destitute or cast adrift. The public liked Diana though because she seemed like a nice person and sprinkled a bit of stardust into public life.

For some reason, conspiracy theorists seem to be rather obsessed by the royal family. The royal family are often depicted in crank conspiracy circles as being like some global Mafia style organisation with a finger in all manner of nefarious goings on and conspiracies.

I suppose this is an obvious consequence of being a wealthy and famous family. However that doesn't mean they are blood drinking lizards from the fourth dimension. Diana conspiracy theories linger on but he most likely explanation for her death was reckless driving to evade paparazzi and she died as a result of injuries sustained in the crash. It seems highly doubtful that Diana was actually murdered by the SAS, MI6 or whoever it is that people accuse.

REBECCA SCHAEFFER

Rebecca Schaeffer was a twenty-one year-old actress in 1989 and starring in the popular CBS sitcom My Sister Sam. Schaeffer was also up for a part in The Godfather III and had appeared in Woody Allen's Radio Days. She seemed destined to use her sitcom fame as a springboard to a movie career - and had even made tentative early steps towards this goal. Schaeffer was an attractive curly haired brunette who once had aspirations to be a model. Though she found that she wasn't tall enough to be a model her talent as an actor more than compensated and her career in Hollywood was highly promising. Schaeffer was intelligent and ambitious and loved by her family and friends.

Rebecca Schaeffer resided in the Fairfax District of Los Angeles and had an apartment in a Mock Tudor house. Although she was making good money from her sitcom she was a fairly down to earth person and wasn't living an extravagant Hollywood life. Schaeffer was more interested in her career and work than fame but tragically it was her fame that would led to her premature death. One day, Schaeffer heard her doorbell and rushed down thinking it was a script she was expecting to be delivered that morning. Instead she found a young man outside the house who turned out to be a fan who had tracked her down. The intercom didn't work so Rebecca had no choice but to go down and see who wanted to talk to her.

The young man was 19 year-old Robert John Bardo. Bardo was from Tuscon and had become obsessed with Schaeffer after watching her in My Sister Sam. He had previously written her a fan letter and she had penned a polite response with 'love Rebecca' at the end. She did this with all fan letters but Bardo, who was clearly not the full shilling, read way more than was intended into this and assumed he now had some sort of special relationship with Schaeffer that no other fan shared.

Bardo was definitely a bit creepy but Schaeffer didn't sense any danger from him when she opened the door. It was probably Bardo's youth that mitigated any sense of threat. He was still a teenager and even younger than she was. Schaeffer signed an autograph for Bardo and then - as politely as she could - cut short the small talk and went back up to her apartment. Bardo left the neighbourhood but he didn't go home. He went to a nearby diner and had some cheesecake. Bardo was simmering with anger because he felt Schaeffer had been indifferent to him and simply got rid of him as fast as she could. He'd long harboured a delusional fantasy that Rebecca Schaeffer would become his girlfriend but that impossible dream was now crushed by harsh reality.

It later transpired that Robert John Bardo was highly disturbed and dangerous. He had once stalked the doomed child peace activist Samantha Smith and tried to get onto the set of My Sister Sam. Bardo was said to be angry at Rebecca Schaeffer because she'd done a love scene in the film Scenes from the Class Struggle in Beverly Hills. This went against the wholesome sitcom image he had of Schaeffer in his warped imagination. Basically, Robert John Bardo was completely crazy. Not only that but he had a gun on him as he sat in the diner eating cheesecake and simmering with anger at how Schaeffer had not been terribly pleased to see him on her doorstep earlier.

Bardo decided to go back to the Mock Tudor House and talk to Schaeffer again. This happened about an hour after he'd first spoken to her. When she answered the door again Rebecca Schaeffer was understandably annoyed and frustrated to see Bardo standing there again. Schaeffer told Bardo that she'd been patient and signed an autograph for him but he was now harassing her and wasting her day with these interruptions. She told Bardo to leave her alone. At this Bardo produced his gun (which he was carrying around in a plastic bag) and shot her in the stomach. Schaeffer sank to the floor holding her stomach in confusion. "Why?" she said to Bardo. Why had he shot her? There was no logical answer to that question. Robert John Bardo was simply a disturbed and dangerous young man. It was probably inevitable that he would do something tragic one day.

A lot of people in the street apparently heard the screams of Rebecca Schaeffer that day. Bardo ran away as fast as he could. Rebecca Schaeffer was taken to hospital but pronounced dead within an hour. Bardo fled back to his home in Tuscon after the murder but was swiftly arrested by the police. One of Bardo's sisters knew that her brother suffered from mental illness and was obsessed with Rebecca Schaeffer. When she heard that Schaeffer had been murdered she immediately suspected her brother and called the police. This was only a day after his fateful encounter with Rebecca Schaeffer.

Bardo confessed to the murder straight away when he was taken into custody. He was found guilty of first degree murder in 1991 and sentenced to life imprisonment without the possibility of parole. Bardo gave an eccentric performance at the trial. When they played the U2 song in court that Bardo had apparently been inspired by, Bardo started singing along and dancing in his seat. It was pretty clear that this man was seriously crazy.

The most chilling thing about this awful case was the ease with which Bardo managed to find out where Schaeffer lived. Bardo had hired a private investigator and the investigator simply found Schaeffer's address through the California Department of Motor Vehicles. Bardo could have actually done this himself and saved some money but he was obviously too stupid to work it out.

The tragic death of Rebecca Schaeffer triggered new anti-stalking laws. As a result of Rebecca's murder, Congress passed the Driver's Privacy Protection Act (which prohibits state Departments of Motor Vehicles from revealing the home addresses of state residents). The damage had already been done though. Bardo gave an interview in prison in which he said that if he had one wish it would be that Rebecca Schaeffer was still alive. Well, it was a bit late for that wasn't it? Maybe you shouldn't have shot her in the first place.

In 2007, Bardo suffered a nasty prison attack in which he was stabbed eleven times. He somehow survived though. At the time of writing, Bardo is still imprisoned at the Avenal State Prison in Avenal, Calif.

Rebecca Schaeffer's boyfriend at the time of her death was the writer and director Brad Silberling. He based his 2002 film Moonlight Mile on her murder. Rebecca was buried at the Ahavai Sholom Cemetery in Portland, Multnomah County, Oregon. The murder of Rebecca Schaeffer remains one of the most chilling examples of 'stalking' ever recorded in Hollywood. It was a horrible and dreadfully sad case. The only crumb of comfort was the fact the fact that Rebecca's death did tighten the law and make such things more difficult to happen in the future. Rebecca's father campaigned for tighter gun control laws in the wake of her death.

Any society that enabled people like Robert John Bardo to easily purchase guns clearly needed to have a serious think about its laws.

JEAN SEBERG

Jean Seberg became famous in 1956 when Otto Preminger chose her out of 18,000 hopefuls to play Joan of Arc in the 1956 film Saint Joan. Seberg, who was from Iowa, was only seventeen. Although her performance in Saint Joan was unfairly panned she had the last laugh on her critics by becoming a stylish icon through her role in Jean-Luc Godard's Breathless. Seberg was most famous for her short hair. To this day if a female celebrity has a short haircut it is sometimes referred to as a Jean Seberg crop. Her other film roles included Paint Your Wagon and The Mouse That Roared with Peter Sellers. Seberg was hip and gamine. She was definitely an icon although more appreciated in Europe than Hollywood. Seberg didn't seem too phased by this and was happy to live in France and make European movies.

Seberg's political views, which included some public support for the Black Panthers, drew the attention of the FBI and their treatment of her was scandalous. The Black Panthers were a revolutionary leftist organisation formed in 1966. The crazy thing about this affair is that all Seberg had done was donate some money to the Black Panthers to support a scheme they had to supply free meals to children in deprived areas. It wasn't as if she was advocating a revolution or taking up arms. She was just trying to help poor kids get a square meal! They say though that no good deed goes unpunished and so it was with Jean Seberg.

Crazy old J Edgar Hoover declared that Seberg must be "neutralized" and so the FBI launched a nasty and shameless smear campaign against her. They put Seberg under surveillance (which made her paranoid) and spread a fake newspaper rumour that father of her impending baby was not her French husband but a Black Panther leader. The FBI memo read - 'The possible publication of Seberg's plight could cause her embarrassment and serve to cheapen her image with the general public'.

Seberg suffered a miscarriage and her mental health declined. She killed herself in 1979 in Paris. She proved that her dead baby was white (thus debunking the Panther story) and sued three publications but the FBI badgered her until she went back to France. Seberg was only forty years-old when she was found dead in her car with mineral water and barbiturates on the seat beside her. She had been missing for ten days when she was found.

Seberg was clearly someone who battled depression but it wouldn't be an overstatement to say that the FBI played a big part in her sadly premature death. When she stayed in a New York hotel once she discreetly put sticky tape on some of the drawers and wardrobes and - sure enough - when she returned found the tape had been disturbed and her stuff rifled through. When Seberg gave an autograph to a fan in the street one time, FBI men searched the girl afterwards and tried to find out what Seberg had said.

At the time of Seberg's death there were stories that someone else might have been present when she died (which would obviously suggest possible foul play) but Seberg's husband (who later committed suicide himself himself) said that she had tried to take her life before several times. Seberg's last brush with Hollywood was in the 1970 film Airport (which starred Burt Lancaster and Dean Martin). After this she mostly made increasingly experimental European films.

SELENA

Selena Quintanilla-Pérez was a Texas born Latino singer who became a huge star in the 1990s. She was hugely popular and famous for her impressive vocal range. She won numerous awards, had great commercial success, and signed with a major label. Selena was known as the queen of Tejano. Fate was intervene in tragic fashion though thanks to Yolanda

Saldívar. Yolanda Saldívar was a former nurse who became obsessed with Selena after attending one of her concerts. Saldívar began badgering Selena's father (who was obviously someone with great influence over his daughter's career and business empire) with requests for permission to start a Selena fan club in San Antonio. Permission for this was eventually granted and Yolanda Saldívar turned the regional fan club into a great success, attracting thousands of members.

As a reward for her efforts, Yolanda Saldívar was taken into the Selena business empire and became her local agent. Saldívar was then put in charge of the chain of fashion boutiques Selena had opened. Though no one knew it at the time it was a huge and eventually tragic mistake to allow Yolanda Saldívar to become part of team Selena. Yolanda Saldívar even moved house to be closer to Selena. Trouble was brewing though because there were soon rumblings of discontent from others in Selena's entourage about Yolanda Saldívar. They simply didn't like Saldívar and they didn't trust her either. This sixth sense turned to be completely on the mark. Yolanda Saldívar, to put it mildly, was bad news and seriously unhinged.

It soon transpired that Yolanda Saldívar had a habit of firing staff members she didn't like in the Selena boutiques - which began to have an effect on sales. Saldívar had grown to enjoy the power she had and was throwing her weight around at every opportunity. Other members of Selena's inner circle grew to dislike Yolanda Saldívar and wanted to get rid of her. Selena's father was among those who wanted to give Saldívar the boot in the end. Selena stood by Yolanda Saldívar out of loyalty but matters came to a head when it was discovered that Saldívar had embezzled thousands of dollars from the boutiques and fan club.

Yolanda Saldívar is said to have stolen about $60,000 through her duties as boutique manager and boss of the Selena fan club. The crimes became apparent when people started writing in and complaining that they had sent their money to join the

Selena fan club but received nothing in return. Unknown to Selena and her family, Yolanda Saldívar had previous when it came to dodgy and criminal deeds. In 1984 she had stolen $9000 from a doctor she worked as a book-keeper for. Saldívar had settled the case out of court and obviously managed to keep this hidden when she was employed by Selena.

On March 31, 1995, in Corpus Christi, Texas, Selena arranged to meet Saldívar at a motel and confronted her with the financial fraud charges. Selana demanded to see financial documents whereupon Yolanda Saldívar produced a handgun and pointed it at Selana. Selena tried to flee but was shot in the back. The bullet severed an artery and exited through Selena's chest. Saldívar then chased the injured Selena down a corridor shouting abuse. Motel staff arrived on the scene and Selena, who was seriously injured and covered in blood, managed to give them Saldívar's name and room number before she passed out.

Though an ambulance only took two minutes to arrive it was already too late because Selena had lost so much blood. Selena collapsed and died in hospital shortly afterwards of blood loss and cardiac arrest. She was only 23 years-old. The doctors said that if the bullet had entered Selena's body a tiniest fraction to either side she probably would have survived. Tragically though the single bullet went in at a crucial spot and caused too much damage.

Yolanda Saldívar tried to get in her car and drive away but after a nine hour stand-off she was captured by police officers and FBI agents. Saldívar sat in the car for hours threatening to shoot herself. Yolanda Saldívar's legal team tried to claim the murder of Selena had been an accident but this didn't stand up to much scrutiny in court. The prosecution pointed out that Yolanda Saldívar was a trained nurse yet made no attempt to offer medical assistance to the wounded Selena - thus confirming that the murder was intentional.

The fact that Saldívar was witnessed chasing Selena down a corridor with a gun also obviously made a mockery of her ridiculous claim that the shooting had been an accident. Saldívar claimed that she had pulled the gun out to shoot herself but Selena had tried to stop her and in the resulting struggle she had accidentally shot the singer. This defence didn't stand up to much scrutiny in court. When the police searched Saldívar's home they found it was a rather creepy shrine to Selena. It appears that Saldívar saw her friendship and influence with Selena about to come to an end and couldn't face up to this. Unfathomably, this resulted in Saldívar murdering her hero.

Saldívar was found guilty of first-degree murder and sentenced to life in prison with the possibility of parole in thirty years. She will be eligible for parole in 2025. Though she has maintained her innocence (she would say that wouldn't she?) and launched several appeals the case was pretty open and shut and no one believed her ludicrous claims that shot Selena by accident.

The murder of Selena was a great shock to her fans and the music industry. It felt as if a great career had been tragically cut short just as it was taking off. Thousands of fans attended Selena's public viewing and mass. Selena was buried at the Seaside Memorial Cemetery in Corpus Christi, TX on April 3, 1995. Selena's family created a foundation and museum in memory and she also received a posthumous Hollywood Star. After her passing, Selena was praised for being a great role model for the Mexican-American community.

ADRIENNE SHELLY

Adrienne Shelly was an actress and director probably best known for her performances in Hal Hartley's The Unbelievable Truth (1989) and Trust (1990) and also the film Waitress. Although she was not quite a huge star she was one of those people that you'd recognise if you saw a picture of her. Adrienne Shelly was a 5'1 strawberry blonde and had a likeable and appealing screen presence. Shelly was highly acclaimed for her work in the film industry and very talented. It seems certain that she would have gone on to become much more famous and give many more great performances in movies. She also appeared in television shows like Homicide: Life on the Street and Oz.

On November 1, 2006 Adrienne Shelly was found dead in the shower of her New York apartment. She was 40 years old. Adrienne Shelly was found hanged in the shower and the police ruled it was a suicide. This verdict was strongly disputed though by her husband Andy Ostroy. He insisted that his wife was perfectly happy and had no reason to take her own life. Ostroy also said that Adrienne Shelly would never have killed herself and left their young two-year old daughter without a mother. The day before her death, Adrienne Shelly had thrown a Halloween party and seemed happy and cheerful. Her career was going great too so why on earth would she suddenly kill herself? It didn't make any sense.

Upon further investigation the police found a sneaker footprint in the bathroom which indicated another person had been present there. The husband of Adrienne Shelly turned out to be right. There was indeed foul play. This case required much more investigating. The sneaker footprint belonged to Diego Pillco, a 19-year-old construction worker from Ecuador. The precise details of what happened were never really established because Pillco changed his story several times while in custody but the general theory seems to be that he was interrupted by Adrienne Shelly while robbing her apartment and then felt he had to silence her to stop her from screaming or alerting the police.

Pillco tried to make it look as if she had committed suicide by hanging her body in the shower. Thankfully, his ruse was uncovered in the end and justice was served. The method of murder was believed to be strangulation - which made the early mistaken verdict of suicide even more puzzling. Pillco pleaded guilty to first-degree manslaughter and was sentenced to 25 years in prison without parole. He will be deported back to Ecuador when his sentence ends. Pillco ended up on a manslaughter rap because the authorities felt this was the safest way to ensure he got a conviction and a lengthy sentence. There is no doubt though that he murdered Adrienne Shelly.

Andy Ostroy later made a documentary in which he celebrated the life of his late wife. Their daughter (who tragically grew up without a mother), now a teenager, also worked on the documentary. It was a profoundly bittersweet experience making the documentary for both of them. Though they were happy and proud to celebrate Adrienne's life it was unavoidably also a sad experience. The most difficult part of the documentary for Ostroy was a scene in which he met the incarcerated Diego Pillco. The family of Adrienne Shelly set up a foundation in her memory. Though sadly gone, her legacy lives on.

NICOLE BROWN SIMPSON

American Football legend OJ Simpson seemed to have the perfect life after he retired from sports. He had wealthy friends, lived in a beautiful house, was sought after for commercials and endorsements, and even began a successful acting career which saw him in appear in films like Capricorn One and The Naked Gun. He had also developed business interests which maintained a regular flow of money and enabled him to live and move in swanky social circles. But behind the scenes, Simpson was not the role model he was made out to be.

His wife Nicole Brown Simpson was terrified of him and the police were regular visitors to their home because of domestic disturbances. Simpson though, who naturally knew all the police officers personally, could usually be relied on to smooth over any trouble with his personal charm and celebrity status.

In 1995, Simpson was charged with the 1994 murders of his ex-wife Nicole Brown Simpson and her friend Ron Goldman - who had been stabbed multiple times. An autopsy determined that Brown had been stabbed seven times in the neck and scalp, and had a 5.5 inches long gash across her throat, which had severed both her left and right carotid arteries and breached her right and left jugular veins. The wound on Brown's neck was so severe it had penetrated a depth of .75 inches into her cervical vertebrae, nearly decapitating her. She also had 'defensive' wounds on her hands. These were brutal murders of the type that serial killer would do.

OJ Simpson was obviously the prime suspect - especially after the infamous Bronco chase. The police also knew he had a violent temper. The case against OJ Simpson seemed fairly clear cut. Blood from the deceased was found in his car. A bloodied glove was also found on his property. Simpson had a motive too as he was prone to anger and jealousy whenever his wife became estranged from him.

Remarkably though, and aided by the racial tensions in Los Angeles at the time because of the Rodney King affair, Simpson's street smart defence team of Johnnie Cochran, Robert Kardashian, Robert Shapiro somehow managed to get Simpson a not guilty verdict. In the wake of the Rodney King incident, there were fears that if OJ was found guilty riots might erupt. This was a possible factor in the verdict. Nonetheless, many were astonished when he was found not guilty.

Cochran in particular made the trial about race. It was their forensic targeting of Police Detective Mark Fuhrman (the man who found much of the evidence that linked Simpson to the crimes) as much as anything that swayed the jury. They discovered that Fuhrman had once openly used racist language in an interview despite denying he hadn't. So,

Fuhrman's testimony retrospectively became suspect and the police case against OJ was portrayed by the defense as a racist stitch-up. It didn't help that the police had not handled the case with the professional competence one might expect, especially when it came to collecting DNA and blood samples.

Simpson returned to his exclusive residence after the trial and resumed playing golf. He tried to get back to his normal life but this proved impossible. He was now a diminished and tainted figure. Many thought he was a murderer. The families of the victims filed a civil suit against him, and in 1997 a civil court awarded a $33.5 million judgement against Simpson for the victims' wrongful deaths. Simpson moved to Florida - a state where a person's residence cannot be seized to collect a debt under most circumstances. Most of his memorabilia was sold and his old friends had abandoned him.

Simpson became a semi-tragic character, doing trashy TV shows (like a Candid Camera clone) and womanising and drinking. OJ wrote a book called If I Did It and even pretended to stab Ruby Wax in a strange documentary about him. In September 2007, a group of men led by Simpson entered a room at the Palace Station hotel-casino and took sports memorabilia at gunpoint, which resulted in Simpson being questioned by police.

In 2008, he was convicted and sentenced to 33 years imprisonment, with a minimum of nine years without parole. It was a fittingly bizarre end to the OJ Simpson story. This was a ludicrously harsh punishment for the sports memorabilia incident and many saw the sentence as retrospective revenge for the murder charges that Simpson had avoided a decade before.

Though he is now free, OJ Simpson remains a tarnished and strange figure - light years away from the man who was once so admired and loved.

DOROTHY STRATTEN

Dorothy Stratten was an actress, model and Playboy playmate. She appeared in the TV shows Buck Rogers in the 25th Century, Fantasy Island, and the bargain basement but mildly cultish 1980 sci-fi film Galaxina. Stratten played a beautiful android in Galaxina and spent the movie in a figure hugging lycra suit that didn't leave much to the imagination. Stratten was very blonde and attractive (in a very 1970s pin-up sort of way - a sort of Charlie's Angel meets Bond girl) and seemed on the cusp of breaking out from her Playboy image and becoming a more mainstream star. She had even begun to appear on the network nightly chat shows as a guest. Stratten got a big break when she won a small part in the Peter Bogdanovich film They All Laughed. Bogdanovich had directed acclaimed films like The Last Picture Show and Paper Moon and was still (just about) at the Hollywood top table at the time.

Bogdanovich had first met Stratten at the Playboy Mansion. He fell in love with Dorothy Stratten and they began an affair. This was likely to have profound and positive consequences for Stratten's career because she was more than likely now going to be in Bogdanovich's movies. Bogdanovich had the clout to turn Dorothy Stratten into a big star and give her more credibility as an actress. The only problem (and it turned out to be an insoluble and ultimately tragic problem) was that Stratten was married to a businessman and hustler named Paul Snider. Snider was a low-life sort of character and rather unstable. He was very ambitious and dangerous and not someone to be taken lightly.

Snider and Dorothy had married in 1979 in Canada. He exerted total control over her career and had no intention of giving up this power. Dorothy Stratten understandably wanted to start a new life with Peter Bogdanovich but Paul Snider was unlikely to make it easy. Dorothy was his meal ticket. It was Snider who had launched Stratten's modelling career in the first place by sending photographs of her to Playboy. Snider felt as if he had created Dorothy Stratten and this gave him a dangerous sense of entitlement over her career and life. It is said that Snider kept turning up on the set of Galaxina and nearly got Dorothy fired because he was such a pain in the neck. Snider had no intention of just allowing Dorothy to walk out of his life.

Though they were separated and Dorothy wanted a divorce, Snider dug his heels in and refused to grant one. He even hired private detectives to follow Dorothy and Peter Bogdanovich around. Snider was pretty furious that this sophisticated hotshot film director had won the heart of Dorothy. He was insanely jealous.

Snider was a pretty odd character. He invented what he called a 'bondage bench' and tried to sell his invention to local sex shops in Los Angeles. He was rather crestfallen when the shops predictably showed no interest in his contraption. By now, Dorothy had moved into the mansion where Peter Bogdanovich lived. You could imagine how Snider felt about this. He was absolutely furious.

Dorothy Stratten eventually arranged to meet Snider in person to ask for a divorce. Stratten had been advised by Bogdanovich and Hugh Hefner not to go and meet Snider but she did so anyway. This would turn out to be a tragic mistake. Dorothy Stratten met Snider in his apartment to discuss the divorce she wanted so desperately. Snider and Stratten used to share this apartment but now Snider was sharing it with others. She took $1,000 in cash to give to Snider in the hope that this might smooth over the meeting and persuade him to agree to the divorce. Sadly though, Snider was in no mood to compromise. This would turn out to be the last day of Dorothy Stratten's life.

The bodies of Dorothy Stratten and Paul Snider were later found by others when they returned to the apartment. Paul Snider had turned up with a shotgun and killed Stratten by shooting her in the face. Part of her cheek had been blown off and she was missing a finger. It was assumed that Dorothy put her hands to her face as Snider pointed the gun and lost a finger when he fired. She was only twenty years-old. Snider then shot himself. It was estimated that Snider killed himself about thirty minutes after he murdered Dorothy.

Dorothy Stratten had also been raped by some sort of bizarre bondage contraption that Snider had set up. She was fastened to the contraption by medical tape. The authorities were apparently never able to establish though if Stratten had been alive or dead when she was sexually assaulted. They felt though it most likely that Dorothy had been alive when she was raped and the act had been done at gunpoint. It seems that Paul Snider realised he had lost Dorothy and now knew she was in love with Peter Bogdanovich. He decided that if he couldn't have Dorothy then no one could.

Peter Bogdanovich was devastated by Dorothy Stratten's death. There was some mud slinging between Bogdanovich and Hugh Hefner after Dorothy died. Bogdanovich seemed to imply that the Playboy 'factory' had damaged Dorothy and got her mixed up with the wrong people. Hefner was rather bemused by the finger pointing and responded by saying - "There is still a great tendency for this thing to fall into the classic cliché of 'smalltown girl comes to Playboy, comes to Hollywood, life in the fast lane,' and that was somehow related to her death. And that is not what really happened. A very sick guy saw his meal ticket and his connection to power, whatever, slipping away. And it was that that made him kill her."

Several years later Peter Bogdanovich raised a few eyebrows by marrying Dorothy's younger sister Louise (who was only twelve when Bogdanovich first met her - though twenty-three when she married him). The marriage lasted until 2001. Two films were made based on this sad case in the wake of Dorothy Stratten's death - Death of a Centerfold: The Dorothy Stratten Story and Star 80 starring Mariel Hemingway.

SHARON TATE

In 1969, Sharon Tate was an actress who had appeared in films like The Fearless Vampire Killers and Valley of the Dolls. Her TV roles had included The Man from U.N.C.L.E. and The Beverly Hillbillies. Her career was obviously boosted by the fact she was now married to the famous film director Roman Polanski. At 26 years of age, Sharon Tate seemed destined to become a huge star. Alas though, fate was to intervene in horrific fashion.

On August 8, 1969, Sharon Tate, who was nine months pregnant, was entertaining some friends at her Hollywood home. Her husband Roman Polanski was away in London making a film. Tate and her friends were subject to one of the most evil and infamous home invasions in history thanks to the orders of the nutty but charismatic cult leader Charles Manson. Manson had sent four of his 'followers' - Linda Kasabian, Tex Watson, Susan Atkins, and Patricia "Katie" Krenwinkel - to go and murder Tate. Tate's friends Jay Sebring, Wojciech Frykowski, and Abigail Folger, who were unfortunate enough to be in the house that night, were also killed.

The Manson cult members had cut the phone lines before they climbed over the walls to the property. Sharon Tate was stabbed nearly twenty times and had one of her breasts cut off. There were stab wounds from her head to her feet. The word 'pig' was scrawled on a door in her blood. This was a horrific attack on innocent people. The victims were beaten, hung, stabbed, shot, and suffered a dreadful ordeal. Charles Manson and three of the assailants were all sentenced to life in prison for this senseless and tragic act. Manson wasn't actually present at the murders but he had issued the instructions and egged on his brainwashed followers to commit these crimes.

'Just what is a cult?' wrote Psychology Today. 'The word itself is controversial, because it used to be used to mean any religious group with unusual beliefs that deviated from the norm, what we might today consider a sect. Today, the term destructive cult is used to describe groups that use manipulative techniques and mind control to heighten suggestibility and subservience. They tend to isolate recruits from former friends and family in order to promote total dependence on the group.

The aim is to advance the goals of the group's leaders, which is to have total control over members. Gaining total control of members is done by assaulting the minds of recruits, an assault meant to control their minds. The mind is located in the brain and in certain hormones and enzymes that travel through the body, affecting our senses. It is through the senses. through seeing, hearing, tasting, smelling and touching. that we know about the world. Think of the body as a giant pharmaceutical factory that manufactures powerful, mind-altering chemicals which we can release by immersing ourselves in mood altering activities or ingesting mood altering substances.

'The medieval Christian mystics who starved and flagellated themselves knew this well. So do Turkey's Whirling Dervishes who once a year, put on long white robes with full skirts, black cloaks, and tall conical red hats and twirl in unison to the sound of drums and flutes, faster and faster, whirling their way toward God and ecstasy. Cults start seducing people with love-bombing, paying a great deal of attention to and being very affectionate with potential recruits. a very effective way of connecting with someone who is feeling lonely and isolated. Then they assault and overwhelm their senses by using various various techniques to induce a dissociated state, an altered state of consciousness, a trance state, in which mind and body are disconnected from each other.

'These techniques include sleep and food deprivation, drumming, chanting, lecturing on and on for hours, flashing lights, spinning around in circles, all of which assault the senses and break down a person's ability to think. The cult uses mind control to fill the dissociated mind with their beliefs and magical thinking. A moment comes when the mind shuts down and seems to snap from this assault to the nervous system. Snapping may happen suddenly and abruptly, or it may be a slower, more gradual process of subtle changes, resulting in personality change. The cult preys upon the tendency of many to rely on magical thinking, which reinforces the tendency to endow the leader with omnipotent and magical powers, much like the child's early mental representations of the parent who at that time, did control his universe. The member can readily come to believe that the leader can read his mind or hear conversations at a distance. Slowly, greater and greater irrational power is attributed to the leader.

'Because the cult leader tends to be a person with a sense of self-esteem so damaged that he requires the adoration, obedience, and subjugation of others to gain a sense of self-esteem and power, he cannot get enough of this This is very much the same dynamic as is found in cases of domestic violence, when one spouse, usually the husband, Tries to assert total control over the other, seemingly a cult of one.

Some in cults who cannot verbally express what they feel about what has been done to them express it through their bodies, harming themselves through cutting and burning themselves, starving their bodies or stuffing themselves with food when they can get their hands on it, or purging through vomiting. When they get of sick in the cult, this is when the cult will eject them because they feel no responsibility for getting them the help they need. It should not be a surprise to hear that many cults are openly against psychotherapy.'

Surprisingly, there seems to be no clear consensus of the type of person who will join a cult. Statistics indicate that very few cult members suffer from major psychological problems. Most cult members are just ordinary people. The reason for this is that cults like to have productive, functioning members who are good at recruiting others or making money for the cult. It doesn't do much good for a cult group if they only recruit dysfunctional people. Cults generally prefer to recruit intelligent well adjusted people. The more destructive cults will then use brainwashing and 'thought reform' on those they have recruited.

Away from his nutty cult group there was literally no one who didn't want Manson locked up for life and that's exactly what happened. Linda Kasabian escaped charges though because she didn't enter the house and an eyewitness for the prosecution. The murders cast a dark cloud over Hollywood. As you might imagine, celebrities greatly increased their security. They hired guard dogs, got bigger gates, and employed private security guards. Many celebrities purchased guns lest they should face something similar.

After he returned from London, Roman Polanski had to be heavily sedated and ended up staying with the film producer Robert Evans. Evans was a friend of Polaski and Sharon Tate and could easily have been at the house that night. He was lucky he wasn't because he would have been murdered. The British actress Joanna Pettet visited Sharon Tate at the house that fateful day and left only hours before the home invasion took place. Talk about a lucky escape.

Manson's plan was to commit horrific crimes to blame on black Americans to incite a race war. This was a plan he named Helter Skelter. Needless to say, Manson was completely crazy. The author Joan Didion wrote of the Sharon Tate murders -

"Many people I know in Los Angeles believe that the Sixties ended abruptly on August 9, 1969, ended at the exact moment when word of the murders on Cielo Drive traveled like brushfire through the community, and in a sense this is true." The murder of Sharon Tate was one of the most brutal and shocking in Hollywood history.

OLIVE THOMAS

Silent film actress Olive Thomas had one of the most bizarre deaths in Hollywood history. She died as a consequence of unwittingly drinking her husband's syphilis medication. This happened in 1920 when she was 25. Olive Thomas was a beautiful star and married to Jack Pickford, an actor and brother of the actress Mary Pickford. One night she drank the mercury bichloride he used for his infection - mistakenly presuming that it was water or even tonic water. She died four days later of poisoning.

There were whispers that she might have committed suicide but these were never proven and, besides, surely she would have thought of a better way to kill herself than an agonising slow death through mercury bichloride poisoning? This story created quite a scandal in Hollywood. In fact you could even say that Olive Thomas was one of the first 'celebrity deaths' to get wide coverage in the media.

The nature of her death caused many to complain that Hollywood was debauched and immoral. A spate of other incidents in Hollywood at this time also attracted the outrage of conservative and religious groups. They thought Hollywood was full of sex fiends and drug addicts. Adding fuel to the fire was the case of Wallace Reid. Reid was one of the biggest stars of the silent era. He made over a hundred short films and seemed set for a long career. He was handsome and athletic and even raced cars in his spare time. Reid was like the big action star of the era and hugely popular.

In 1919, while shooting The Valley of the Giant, Reid was injured in a train crash. In order to keep the actor free of pain and able to work, he was prescribed morphine. Reid became hopelessly addicted to morphine and used it to suppress the pain he still felt from his injuries. He made more films but with his drug addiction beginning to spiral out of control, he died in 1922 at the age of 31. The great tragedy for Reid is that he was recklessly given copious amounts of morphine in an era when drug rehabilitation was nowhere near as professional or widespread as it would later become.

Another scandal involved William Taylor. Taylor was a very successful director in Old Hollywood but his death is a mystery that has yet to be solved. He was said to be one of the first advocates of what is known as the casting couch. If you wanted to be in one of his films you had a better chance if you slept with him. He also liked young girls and didn't care if they were of legal age.

Taylor was found dead in his office but one knows who murdered him. It could be that it was a relative of one of the young starlets he took advantage of. Legend has it that the police removed evidence of Taylor's contacts and liaisons to spare studio blushes. He was known to have connections to crime figures so this added another potential line of inquiry into his murder. We simply don't know who killed him though.

The most famous Hollywood scandal of this time came in 1921. The comedian 'Fatty' Arbuckle held a party in his hotel suite and a woman there named Virginia Rappé fell ill, dying four days later from peritonitis. Arkbuckle was arrested and charged with manslaughter with lurid stories swirling around that he'd assaulted the woman and was some sex crazed monster in real life. He was in fact completely innocent and acquitted in six minutes at the final trial. Hollywood was reluctant to put Arbuckle's name on anything afterwards officially but he did direct films under an assumed name and work with Chaplin and Keaton again and many others who stood by him. He was eventually offered a three film contract by a studio and died a happy - and innocent - man.

Many accounts of Arbuckle disregard the fact that he was cleared of any charges and received an apology from both the courts and the film industry before he died.

THELMA TODD

Thelma Todd was a blonde actress known as Hot Toddy and The Ice Cream Blonde who famously appeared in the Marx Brothers films Horse Feathers and Monkey Business. Her last film was The Bohemian Girl with Laurel & Hardy. She appeared in 120 shorts and movies and was an infamous girl around town known for a fast lifestyle and colourful love life. Todd made a fantastic foil for Groucho Marx and was a pretty accomplished performer. She was sort of like the Marilyn Monroe of her day with her blonde pin-up girl looks. Todd was a former Miss Massachusetts on the pageant circuit but in real life she was not your stereotypical dim blonde bimbo at all and had once attended a teacher training college. Todd was spotted by Hollywood talent scouts though and so instead of becoming a teacher she headed for Hollywood and became an actress.

Todd owned an eatery in Malibu called Thelma Todd's Sidewalk Cafe and it became a popular place for celebrities and hipsters of the era to hang out. She had got into the restaurant business because she didn't plan to be an actress forever. Thelma knew her looks would fade in the end and the studios would inevitably replace her with someone younger so she wanted to have something else to do when that time came. In 1935, at the age of 29, Todd was found dead behind the wheel of a car in her garage. The garage belonged to her business partner and occasional lover Roland West. Todd and West actually lived in an apartment above the eatery. Believe it or not, West's estranged wife Jewel Carmen lived there. It was West and Carmen who started the business in the first place.

The official verdict on Thelma Todd's death was carbon monoxide poisoning and it was presumed that this was either suicide or an accident. However, some movie historians and people at the time believe that Todd might have been murdered. Blood was found on her mouth and a second autopsy did not happen because her body was cremated. The Chicago Tribune claimed that Thelma Todd was found with two cracked ribs and a broken nose. If this was the case then it seems unlikely to have been a simple case of suicide. Todd could hardly had done these injuries to herself. Even if she fell forward or sideways in the car after she passed it's hard to see how these serious injuries could have happened.

The day after Todd's death a newspaper published an article in which it suggested foul play and revealed that Todd had been the victim of extortion threats demanding money. Who the extortion threats came from was not stipulated and presumably unknown (obviously, an extortionist is unlikely to sign their name on a threatening letter). Suspects in Todd's death include Pat DiCicco, who was Todd's ex-husband. He had mob links and was known to have been violent to Todd in the past. Pat DiCicco is said to have felt betrayed and humiliated when Todd left him so he had a motive.

The mobster Lucky Luciano is also a suspect. Luciano had a relationship with Todd that was said to be stormy and obstreperous. It is said that Luciano wanted Todd to open a casino in her restaurant but she had dug her heels in and refused to do this. As you might imagine, this didn't make him very happy. Hollywood gossip suggested that Luciano had got Todd hooked on drugs and was determined to maintain influence over her. A mob boss would patently be capable of having Todd killed and making it look like a suicide so Lucky Luciano was an obvious suspect in this suspicious death.

Jewel Carmen is also sometimes dubbed a suspect. Carmen apparently threatened Todd a few times because she was angry that the restaurant wasn't making much money. Carmen probably wasn't too thrilled either to see that her estranged husband was attracted to Todd. The alleged motive for Carmen is presumably jealousy more than anything. Roland West is also a suspect in Todd's death although - in mitigation - his grief seemed genuine enough when her body was found. The motive in this theory is that West was jealous of Todd's numerous affairs and boyfriends.

Believe it or not, Thelma Todd's mother Alice is even a suspect. Alice Todd was the main financial beneficiary of Thelma's early death. Alice Todd had began preparations to build herself a house before Thelma died despite having no visible means to fund such a project. Thelma's death naturally gave Alice the financial means to build her house. This is what you might describe as a convenient and rather suspicious turn of events.

One thing that goes against this theory though is that Alice was pretty vocal at the time in declaring that her daughter had been murdered. If she had murdered Thelma you'd think she'd want to go along with the suicide theory to cover her tracks - unless it was all a cunning double bluff. Alice Todd seems like a long shot when it comes to potential murder suspects. She probably would have been the least likely to have done this (if indeed it was even a murder in the first place).

One theory concerning Todd's death is that she had accidentally locked herself out after a night on the town and decided to sit in her car in the garage to keep warm and somehow accidentally killed herself by putting the engine on. The day she died, Thelma had been late getting home from a party and had been dropped off around 3am. The counter to this argument is that people in this era were warned a lot about carbon monoxide poisoning with cars and Thelma was pretty intelligent and so would have been aware of these dangers herself. It could be though that her logic that night was clouded by alcohol.

One factor which counters the suicide theory is that Todd was apparently very happy at the time of her death. There was no sign of depression or unhappiness. Thelma died during production of the 1936 Laurel & Hardy film The Bohemian Girl. Most of Todd's scenes in the movie were cut by the producer Hal Roach after her death but as a tribute one scene of her singing Heart of a Gypsy was kept intact.

JACK UNTERWEGER

Jack Unterweger was an Austrian serial killer born in 1950. His was a story so strange you couldn't make it up. In 1976 he was convicted for murdering a sex worker and sent to prison. Unterweger wrote an autobiography in prison where he talked about his awful childhood and how he was now reformed and should be released. He attracted liberal criminal reform supporters who were charmed by his book and in 1990 he was released - becoming something of a celebrity and appearing on talk shows. A film about him was soon planned and he became a journalist. The only problem was that he wasn't really reformed. He soon started killing again!

Unterweger was plainly dodgy from a young age. He had many convictions for theft but also for 'pimping' and sexual assault. He spent several years in prison in the late 60s and early 70s. In 1974 he strangled a German teenager to death by means of her own bra. He was sentenced to life in prison - whereupon he became a prolific writer of poems and stories. Most saliently, he wrote an autobiography titled Purgatory or The Trip to Prison – Report of a Guilty Man. A campaign soon began to get Unterweger released from prison. The campaign was supported by Elfriede Jelinek, the Austrian playwright who later won the 2004 Nobel Prize in Literature.

The Austrian historian Peter Huemer, another famous figure hoodwinked by Unterweger, said - "Unterweger represented the great hope of intellectuals that, through the verbalisation of problems, you can somehow get to grips with them. We wanted to believe him very badly. At the time, I genuinely believed that Unteweger was a reformed man." The campaign was successful and Jack Unterweger was released from prison in 1990. Guess what? This turned out to be a very big mistake.

Upon his release, Unterweger staged plays, lectured schoolchildren about crime, went on television chatshows, and worked as a reporter for the Austrian version of the BBC.

While he was living the life of riley as a celebrity and being feted by Austrian literary folks, Unterweger secretly picked up where he left of and started murdering women again.
He would target lone sex workers and was a very sadistic killer. Many of the victims had puncture wounds in their buttocks and severe head damage. He would usually finish the victim off by strangulation. His initial (fresh) murders were in Czechoslovakia and Austria. He was then giving an assignment writing about crime in Los Angeles.

While Unterweger was in Los Angeles, three sex workers were strangled to death. The police in Los Angeles investigating these crimes learned that a certain Austrian journalist who had a previous murder conviction for strangling a sex worker was in the city. They placed Unterweger under surveillance and eventually arrested him in Miami. He was sent back to Austria and charged with eleven murders. As you can imagine, those people who campaigned for his release must have felt pretty stupid by now. On 29 June 1994, he was sentenced to life in prison without the possibility of parole. That night, Jack Unterweger hung himself in prison.

FRED WEST

Frederick Walter Stephen West was born in 1941 in Herefordshire. 25 Cromwell Street in Gloucester later became an infamous address in English criminal history thanks to the barely believable antics of Fred and Rose West. This bizarre couple were involved in murder (which included some of their own children), prostitution, rape, and incest. Fred West was the second of eight children. He grew up in poor rural conditions and left school at fifteen to labour on the farm. West could not read or write very well. When he was a teenager, West had a bike accident which left him with a metal plate in his head. He also picked up another head injury when he fell from some stairs. Fred West was no genius even before the head injuries so you can imagine what he was like after them.

Despite looking like an exhibit in a horror waxworks, Fred West considered himself to be a very suave ladies man. In reality, he was a creep who molested a number of underage girls. In 1961 he got a thirteen year-old girl pregnant and had to leave home. He was cleared of rape but found guilty of molestation. West married a Scottish woman named Catherine Costello soon after and they had a daughter named Charmaine. This was not West's biological daughter. Fred West rarely seemed to be the biological father of his children. Fred West, incredibly given that he was convicted child molester, got a job driving an ice cream van in Scotland. When he was an ice-cream man, West killed a boy that he ran over by accident. He was nearly lynched and literally had to flee the area and never return.

Fred West had another child with Costello and then they moved to Gloucestershire. Costello's friend Anne McFall moved in with them but then Fred West's wife departed and left him with McFall. McFall fell pregnant with Fred West's child and she wanted to get married. Fred West's response to the marriage suggestion was to murder her. He burried Anne in the caravan park where they lived - but not before cutting her toes off. West had a grisly habit of removing the toes and fingers of his victims.

In 1968, Fred West met sixteen year-old Rose Letts. She would of course become infamous as Rose west. Fred west was 27 when they got together. Rose was a woman of fairly low intelligence who had a dismal childhood. It is often reported that she suffered sexual abuse from her father. Rose is suspected of killing Fred West's daughter Charmaine in 1971 while he was in prison. Catherine Costello returned at this time to try and get her children back so Fred West murdered her.

Fred and Rose were married in 1972 and moved to 25 Cromwell Street. This was a three floor house with a cellar and back garden. The cellar of 25 Cromwell Street was (no surprise here) turned into a sex dungeon by Fred West. In 1972, Caroline Owens was hired as a babysitter by Fred and Rose West. She said she blacked out and woke up to find Fred West binding her with tape. She escaped and went to the police but they didn't seem to believe her story. Fred West escaped with a mild slap on the wrist because Owens was so scared of him she refused to take the Wests to court.

The Wests took in some lodgers around this time. Fred West (unsurprisingly) drilled peep holes into his walls so he could spy on the lodgers. West was also sexually abusing his daughters. The West children went to the hospital dozens of times for injuries they had sustained. One of the victims of Fred and Rose West around this time was Lucy Partington. Lucy was a cousin of the writer Martin Amis. She was abducted and murdered. The Wests turned the top floor of their house into a brothel so that Rose could work as a prostitute.

Fred West would secretly film her sessions with clients. Fred and Rose were into sadomasochism. They had several more children and continued to kill. The children would later say that they remembered strange incidents where their parents made them hide in a box. It is presumed they did this so the children would not see them disposing of a body.

Fred West's daughter Heather resisted Fred West's sexual advances so she was killed and buried in the garden. In his confession to the police, Fred West complained that Rose West had initially stuffed the body of one of his daughters in a dustbin. He was talking about Heather. In the early 1990s, the social services heard stories about Fred West sexually abusing his daughters so passed the information onto the police. The police arrested Fred and Rose West for the rape of a minor (Rose was charged with assisting the rape). When the police watched the family home videos the Wests had shot of outings to the zoo and parks they noticed that a child seemed to be missing. This was Heather. Fred West said Heather had left home but the police could find no evidence that Heather's national insurance number had been used. She hadn't got a job or claimed any government welfare. She had literally vanished.

The police obtained legal permission to search the house. When the police dug up the West garden and cellar in 1994 they discovered nine bodies. The victims were young women and West children. The bodies at 25 Cromwell Street were buried in the cellar, garden, and under the patio. Fred West was a plasterer by trade - which must have come in handy when he was trying to hide bodies. When the horrors of Cromwell Street were revealed, the neigbours of Fred and Rose West expressed astonishment that these two seemingly placid people could be capable of murder. 25 Cromwell Street was dubbed the House of Horrors by the British media.

Fred West confessed to the murders and told the police where his first wife Rena, Anna McFall and daughter Charmaine were buried. Rose West claimed to be innocent but this was never credible. She was actually vital in allowing Fred West to pick up a number of victims. The presence of a wife made him seem like a normal (as far as the werewolf like Fred West could ever appear normal) person rather than a threat. Fred West was charged for twelve murders but hung himself in 1995 before the trial. Fred West hung himself in custody by making a rope from bedsheets he had tied together. He was 53 years-old.

Rose West received life in prison at her 1995 trial. The couple had lured young women with the promise of a babysitting job or room to rent and then killed them. The fact they had killed a number of their own children too made the case even more disturbing and unexplainable. Gloucester City Council demolished 25 Cromwell Street in 1996 and replaced it with a public walkway. When 25 Cromwell Street was demolished by the council, there was a dispute over the iron sign with the house number. The council wanted to melt it down and destroy it but some West relatives (for reasons best known to themselves) wanted to keep it. Of the Wests' surviving children, one committed suicide and two others have attempted suicide. One can scarcely comprehend the misery and horror they must have encountered in their childhood.

NATALIE WOOD

On November 29, 1981, the actress Natalie Wood was on a boating trip with her famous actor husband Robert Wagner. Wood and Wagner had actually divorced and remarried. Also on the yacht was another actor - Christopher Walken. At the time Wood and Walken were shooting a sci-fi film called Brainstorm together. Wood had almost completed her scenes for the movie and only had a few left to shoot. They were all on Robert Wagner's boat Splendour. After a night of drinking, Natalie apparently left the boat and her dead body was later found off Catalina Island, near Los Angeles. The 43 year-old Natalie Wood had drowned. She was wearing a nightgown and socks - which hardly seems like swimming attire. Her death was ruled an accident but bruises were later found on her body - which suggested foul play.

Natalie Wood first came to prominence as a child actor in Miracle on 34th Street. She was later nominated for an Oscar three times. By 1983, Natalie Wood's career wasn't as hot as it used to be (Hollywood is notorious for losing interest in actresses over 40) but she had recently received the Golden Globe Award for Best Actress in Television Series Drama for her performance in the miniseries From Here to Eternity. There was no reason to doubt that her acting chops would see her secure many good parts in the future.

The night in question, Wood, Wagner, and Walken had gone ashore to have dinner and returned to the boat around 10pm. They were all said to be mildly intoxicated from the drinks they had enjoyed that evening. Robert Wagner said that Natalie retired to their cabin at around 10-45pm but when he went to join her he found that she was gone. Wagner said he had spent some time chatting to Walken before he went to see his wife. Upon noticing that the dinghy was missing, Wagner said he alerted the authorities (the Harbor Patrol and Coast Guard). A police helicopter found Natalie's drowned body the next morning. Wagner's account of that night and his actions has been disputed ever since. Not everyone believed he was telling the truth.

Dennis Davern, who was the captain of the yacht that night, later said that Wagner and Walken had a blazing argument that night during which Wagner accused him of wanting to have sex with his wife. Davern further claimed that Wagner showed no interest whatsoever in looking for Natalie Wood after she went overboard. Davern assumed that Wood had taken the dinghy ashore after an argument with her husband. The dinghy in question was found near Natalie Wood's body when she was discovered. Robert Smith, the captain of the rescue boat on duty at the time, said he found Robert Wagner's attitude strange at the time. He claimed that Wagner had not immediately reported Natalie's disappearance.

John Corina, a lieutenant in the Los Angeles Sheriff's Department Homicide Bureau, said in 2011 that new witnesses had come forward in the case. These witnesses were on boats moored near the Splendour at the time. They reported hearing a ferocious argument from Wagner's yacht that night. This evidence supported the claims of Dennis Davern. Natalie's sister Lana Wood (who played Plenty O'Toole in the Bond film Diamonds Are Forever) remains convinced that Wagner knows more than he has confessed to and might have murdered her sister. Robert Wagner has dismissed claims of foul play as preposterous and was never charged with anything. The investigation into Natalie wood's death later suggested that she could have picked up some of her injuries before she went in the water.

The official verdict remains ambiguous and her death was put down to 'drowning and other undetermined factors'. One thing that is clear is that Natalie Wood had been drinking that night so was in no fit state to swim ashore or pilot a dinghy. It could be that in her intoxicated state she underestimated how difficult it would be to get ashore. Though it could all have been a tragic accident the suspicion surround Wagner's participation has never completely gone away. As for Christopher Walken, well, Walken has (unsurprisingly perhaps) rarely spoken about the tragedy. In his few recorded comments on the tragedy he said it was just a random accident.

One theory is that Wagner might have lowered the dinghy himself to make it look like Natalie Wood left the boat of her own free will. Wood was said to be scared of water - which would appear to make it unlikely that she would willingly climb into a dinghy alone and at night. Dennis Davern also claimed that Wagner refused to turn the boat's lights on to scan the water when it became apparent that Natalie Wood was gone. It should be stressed that Robert Wagner has never been charged with anything and believes any suggestion he had a hand in Natalie Wood's tragic death is completely preposterous. His grief at the funeral certainly seemed genuine too.

However, John Corina has said that attempts by the police to interview Wagner about the case were persistently frustrated by Wagner's lawyers. Robert Wagner would probably argue that he spoke to the police at the time and has nothing more to say. In recent years Suzanne Finstad wrote a biography of Natalie wood in which she claimed that a doctor who examined Wood's body found friction burns consistent with being pushed while trying to hold onto something. The short version of this is that Finstad believes Robert Wagner pushed Natalie off the boat. It seems like the mystery of Natalie wood's death will continue to keep armchair detectives busy for some time to come.

AILEEN WUORNOS

Aileen Wuornos was born in Rochester, Michigan, in 1956. Wuornos is another serial killer who was born under a full moon. Aileen Wuornos is arguably the most famous female serial killer thanks to a film and documentary which ere made about her crimes. She killed seven men in total from 1989 to 1990. Wuornos had an abusive upbringing at the hands of a strict grandfather. Wuornos was a surprisingly beautiful child but a tough life obviously extracted a cruel toll on her looks in the end. She was homeless at fifteen and sold her body to survive. Tired of the cold, she eventually hitch-hiked to Florida and married a rich man. The marriage only lasted days. He put a restraining order on her because Wournos would beat him up. Aileen Wuornos was a notoriously volatile person with an unpredictable (and rather frightening) temper.

After her marriage collapsed, Aileen Wuornos worked as a prostitute and, in desperate need of money, turned to murder. She picked up her victims on the I-75 highway. She would always target middle-aged men in nice cars. Wuornos would start to undress in the car and ask the driver to pull over somewhere secluded. Then she would get out of the car and shoot them before stealing their wallets. Aileen Wuornos would often shoot her victims multiple times.

Her alleged motivation for the murders was that she wanted to support her girlfriend and lover Ty. One might argue that a hatred of men was rather evident too. Psychologist Marissa Harrison concluded from her study that female serial killers were mostly motivated by material gain whereas male serial killers were mostly motivated by sexual urges. Aileen Wuornos was clearly motivated by her desperate desire to get quick money. Wuornos never really did much to hide the bodies of the victims. They were found fairly quickly and easily. A few men had a lucky escape from Aileen Wuornos. One man actually saw the gun in her purse and managed to drive away.

Aileen Wuornos was captured when the police finally managed to get an accurate artists impression of the killer. Once this sketch was circulated, they soon had a lot of calls telling them the illustration looked like Aileen Wuornos - an angry and violent local woman who seemed to spend most of her time drinking beer in biker bars. Wuornos was taken into custody and the police discovered that she had sold the belongings (like wristwatches and jewellery) of the victims in local pawn shops. Any money they had she of course kept for herself.

Aileen Wuornos claimed that she had killed the men in self-defence because they all tried to rape her. This was seen as a weak and improbable defence. It appeared unlikely that seven different men all tried to rape her at different times on the exact same stretch of highway. One of the victims was selling Bibles and another was a former police chief. They were ordinary people with no criminal history. The fact that Wuornos had not reported a single one of these incidents and always tried to hide the bodies also made her defence seem less than plausible.

Aileen Wuornos eventually pleaded guilty to five murders because she wanted the death penalty. She was tired of prison and court. Aileen Wuornos felt betrayed and alone in the end. Even her beloved girlfriend Ty secretly taped their phone conversations and testified against her. Wuornos became a born again Christian after her conviction. She always got offended when someone called her a serial killer. Aileen Wuornos claimed she was not a serial killer because she never tortured or mutilated her victims. While this was true she did shoot dead several innocent men!

Aileen Wuornos was executed in 2002. Wuornos declined a last meal before her execution and asked for black coffee. For $15 on crime collectible websites you can buy a photograph of Aileen Wuornos posing with a friend before her execution. She looks surprisingly happy in the photo considering the circumstances in which it was taken. Aileen Wuornos was a twist on the common serial killer situation in that she was a prostitute but a killer rather than a victim. She said she wasn't evil but just had a consuming hatred for the human race.

MALCOLM X

Malcolm X was born as Malcolm Little on May 19, 1925 in Omaha, Nebraska. Malcolm's father, Earl Little, was a leader in an African-American group called the UNIA. This made the family a target for racists and they even had their house burned down. Malcolm's father was then found dead on some streetcar tracks when Malcolm was eight years-old. The official verdict was an accident but the family - with good cause you'd imagine - suspected foul play. There wasn't much chance though of black folks getting fair justice in this era. The police and authorities were unlikely to put themselves through too much bother over the death of a black man. This was, sadly, a time of segregation and open racism.

The Little family had a hard time during the Great Depression and Malcolm spent some time in social care. He ended up moving to Boston and spent some in prison after he was caught handling stolen goods. Despite his background and troubles though he was very intelligent and articulate. Malcolm was someone who had a lot to give but no outlet for his talents. This would - for better or worse - soon change though. Malcolm then heard about a political and religious group called the Nation of Islam and became interested. He felt like this was his destiny at last.

The Nation of Islam (often known as the Black Muslims) believed that black people would always be oppressed by whites and that they (black people) were superior. The Nation also believed that Islam was the true faith for people of colour. Malcolm was very taken with these ideas and joined the group. He changed his name to Malcolm X and became the leader of Temple Number 7 in Harlem. Malcolm became close friends with the Nation's new convert - the young heavyweight boxer

Muhammad Ali (Ali was called Cassius Clay before he joined the Nation of Islam). Joining the Nation of Islam made Muhammad Ali very unpopular at the time. He was seen as a loudmouth egomaniac with nothing to back it up.

When he converted to the Nation Of Islam, Muhammad Ali officially became public enemy number one. Ali would surprise everyone though by beating the world heavyweight champion Sonny Liston. No one one was more surprised than Elijah Muhammad when Ali won. Naturally, Elijah didn't admit this. He pretended that he'd predicted an Ali victory all along and that the victory was god's will. You could probably argue that Ali was a useful idiot for the Nation of Islam. Elijah Muhammad's son Herbert was Ali's manager for the duration of his boxing career and took a third of his purses.

Because he was such a charismatic man and speaker, the fame of Malcom X quickly grew. If you catch an old clip of Malcom X being interviewed you find yourself becoming slightly entranced by the quiet force of his personality. Malcom became something of a celebrity - even beyond the Nation of Islam. One might argue that Malcom even became more famous than the Nation's leader Elijah Muhammad. Elijah Muhammad obviously wasn't too happy about this.

The Nation's leader Elijah Muhammad was born Elijah Poole on October 7, 1897, in Sandersville, Ga. He was the son of sharecroppers and slaves and moved to Detroit where he became interested in the ideas of Wallace D. Fard, who had founded the Nation of Islam. Fard preached that a race war was coming and gave his followers Arabic names. Wallace D. Fard simply vanished without trace one day. Attempts to find out who he really was have remained vague to say the least. He was a mysterious and enigmatic figure.

Elijah Muhammad succeeded Fard as the leader of the Black Muslims in 1934. The Nation of Islam believed that white men were 'devils' and that black people were the 'chosen ones' of Allah. They wanted a segregated independent nation for black people to be founded on land in the United States or elsewhere. The Nation of Islam believed that white people were created 6000 years ago by Doctor Yacub. Yacub, according to Fard, was born 20 miles from Mecca in the year 8400BC. He was eventually imprisoned and then banished into exile. Leading 59,999 of his disciples to the island of Pean in the Aegean Sea, he created a new race from the germs of black people. They had fur, were born with tails and walked on all fours. They were white; and they were devils.

It would probably be fair to say that the Nation of Islam had some beliefs which you could describe as barking mad. The most bizarre belief of the Nation of Islam was that a spaceship was going to arrive on Earth one day to 'save' all the black people and leave the white 'devils' to perish. This was Ezekiel and the wheel in the sky - the 'Mother' of all planes. It was crazy stuff. Though a bit creepy, Elijah Muhammad was a passionate and fiery preacher and instilled discipline into his followers. Although his views were deemed divisive, eccentric and racist by many, he moderated them over time and argued that he was seeking to give black people a sense of respect and self-reliance. He always remained though a deeply controversial man.

Critics of Elijah Muhammad argued that segregation was no answer to anything and believed a society where people of all races, colours, and faiths were equal and lived together in harmony and respect should be the true quest. Elijah Muhammad believed he was there to instill self-respect into black people. He wanted them to dress smartly and look after one another. Malcolm X was drawn to the Nation of Islam not only because he liked this doctrine of self-respect but also because he was dubious about the mainstream civil rights movement. Malcolm didn't want integration but rather a separate state for African-Americans to run themselves.

In time though, tension between Malcolm X and the Nation of Islam became apparent. Elijah Muhammad banned him from speaking for ninety days after Malcolm commented that it was a case of "chickens coming home to roost" after the assassination of President John F. Kennedy. Elijah Muhammad was angered by Malcolm's comment because he felt it was bad for the Nation's public relations at this sensitive time for any member of the Nation of Islam to make a political statement about Kennedy's death. Malcolm is then said to have turned against Elijah Muhammad when he learned that the leader was having affairs with young women (which went against what the Nation preached). Malcolm also, over time, came to change his views about race and politics.

Malcolm X eventually left the Nation of Islam and adopted a more mainstream Islamic belief. He no longer believed in racial segregation and seemed to have lost faith in Elijah Muhammad. "The thing that you have to understand about those of us in the Black Muslim movement was that all of us believed 100 percent in the divinity of Elijah Muhammad," he said. "We believed in him. We actually believed that God, in Detroit by the way, that God had taught him and all of that. I always believed that he believed in himself. And I was shocked when I found out that he himself didn't believe it."

Malcolm became a critic of the Nation of Islam and came to believe that equality rather than segregation should be the goal. Malcolm said he had come to realise that there were Muslims of all colours and races. He said that he regretted the fact that he had snubbed white students who wanted to help him fight racism in the past simply because they were white. As you might imagine, Elijah Muhammad didn't take too kindly to Malcolm leaving the movement and speaking up independently. The Nation of Islam wanted Malcolm X to remain silent. To this end they burned down his house.

On February 21, 1965, Malcolm was preparing to give a speech at Manhattan's Audubon Ballroom. A man rushed forward and shot him in the chest with a shotgun. There were twenty-one bullet (and buckshot) wounds on Malcolm's body when he was pronounced dead shortly after. He was thirty-nine years-old. When Malcolm was assassinated, three members of the Nation of Islam were arrested for his murder. The three men were sentenced to life in prison. They all earned parole in the end and all insisted they were innocent. Elijah Muhammad seemed to crow about the death of Malcolm X in a speech but denied the Nation of Islam had anything to do with the murder.

Elijah Muhammad died in 1975 at the age of 77. After his death, his movement split in two. His other son became leader and made them more of a mainstream Islamic movement but Elijah Muhammad's founding principles were continued in an offshoot group (which retained the name Nation of Islam) led by the controversial Louis Farrakhan. Muhammad Ali went with the more moderate wing and became a beloved icon in the 1970s. It's probably not an understatement to say that Ali became the most beloved celebrity in the world - which was a remarkable (and deserved) achievement given his unpopularity in the 1960s in mainstream America.

Many decades later, the men convicted of killing Malcolm were exonerated and their trial ruled retrospectively dubious. The real truth of Malcolm's murder though is almost impossible to discern. The case is very muddied and confusing. There is a theory that the CIA and FBI may have been involved in his death. Friends of Malcolm said there were plenty of cops in the vicinity when he was murdered but none of them offered any protection or seemed especially active even when he was shot. You could probably say that was rather suspicious. Furthermore it has been alleged that key members of Malcolm's security staff were arrested on various charges days before he was shot. The presumed implication is that the authorities wanted Malcolm's security to be as light as possible to make him more vulnerable.

ANTON YELCHIN

Russian born Hollywood actor Anton Yelchin was a young man who seemed destined for even greater stardom than he'd already attained. He was best known for playing Chekov in the rebooted Star Trek film franchise and had carved out a niche playing the young lead in horror flicks like Fright Night and Burying the Ex. He was also the young Kyle Reese in Terminator Salvation. Yelchin had a likeable everyman quality on the screen and he clearly had the acting cops to take on more mature and complex roles when he aged out of the young lead parts. Perhaps his best role was in the thriller Green Room. He was clearly a very talented actor. He also appeared in indie movies and short films. Yelchin wanted to be a director himself and had plans in place to direct his first movie. He was also in a band and loved music.

Yelchin's parents were figure skaters from Leningrad who fled the Soviet Union (then on its last legs) because they felt persecuted for being Jews. They felt that Anton would have a better life if he was born in the United States and they turned out to be right about that. Anton said his parents made great sacrifices to give him a better life than they'd had but the effort seemed to be worth it in the end. Sadly though, tragedy struck just when everything seemed to be going so well.

On June the 19th, 2016, friends of the twenty-seven year-old actor became worried when he didn't turn up to a rehearsal (it was most unlike Anton not to be punctual and show up for his appointments) and so went to his home in the hills of Studio City, California to see what the problem was. They were met with a tragic scene. Yelchin was dead and pinned between a stone pillar and his Grand Cherokee jeep in the driveway.

Yelchin had been on his way to the rehearsal and left the jeep at the top of a slope with the engine running. Why he got out of the car is not known. Maybe he'd forgotten something and wanted to go back for it. It appears that Yelchin did not put the parking brake on (the other explanation is a mechanical fault in the car) and while he was behind the vehicle (and obviously oblivious to potential danger) the 2.5 ton vehicle rolled back and crushed him against a pillar. He must have been caught unaware and had no time to escape.

It is believed that Yelchin was killed almost instantly. His lungs were crushed and the official cause of death was blunt traumatic asphyxia. There were no suspicious circumstances. The death was simply a freak accident. The vehicle involved was among some Fiat Chrysler models under a recall notice for transmission errors leading to unintended rolling. These cars were obviously pretty dangerous and should have been recalled sooner.

One of the ironic things about this tragic death is that Yelchin was known to be one of the more level headed and down to earth actors in Hollywood. He didn't take drugs or lead a party lifestyle. When he wasn't acting he liked to indulge his passion for photography. He seemed like one of the last people in Hollywood you'd predict would die young. Out of respect for Yelchin, the producers of the new Star Trek series said they would not recast the part of Chekov. Star Trek Beyond came out shortly after his death and was dedicated to his memory. At the time of his death Yelchin had five movies in post-production. He was one of the busiest young actors in Hollywood.

Yelchin was buried at the Hollywood Forever Cemetery. Three years earlier, Yelchin had shot a scene at the Hollywood Forever Cemetery for the Joe Dante horror flick Burying the Ex. Spookily, if you watch that film now you can see Yelchin in a scene near where his own grave would soon be. In 2017, a statue of Yelchin was unveiled at his grave. All in all it was a very sad death because Anton Yelchin was only at the beginning of what promised to be an amazing career. Alas, we'll never know now what he would have gone on to do.

After the death of Anton Yelchin, the director Joe Dante said - "I don't believe we'll ever realise the dimensions of the tragedy of his inexplicable loss. I can honestly say I never enjoyed working with an actor more than I did with Anton. Dedicated, curious, optimistic and completely engaged. He'd come to set even when he wasn't working. Sometimes you meet people who you just click with – and we certainly did. His insatiable quest to see every old movie extant was just one of the traits that endeared him to me and reminded me of myself at his age. But acting was only one of his interests – he was a talented photographer and musician, and he was getting ready to direct his first movie. That's what I mean about the extent of our loss. Anton had a terrific future ahead of him, and his loss is our loss. I was proud to be even a small part of what will come to be known as his legacy. And I miss him."

CPSIA information can be obtained
at www.ICGtesting.com
Printed in the USA
BVHW091756060822
643973BV00012B/1350

9 798201 918866